The Allergy
Cookie Jar

The Allergy
Cookie Jar

by Carol Rudoff
foreword by Donald L. Unger, M.D.

Published in the United States by Prologue Publications
First edition

Library of Congress Catalog Card Number: 85-60322
ISBN: 0-930048-14-8

Inquires should be addressed to:

Prologue Publications
P. O. Box 640
Menlo Park, CA 94026

To Neil and Jim
because they created and tested many of the recipes
that went into the making of this volume

Contents

Foreword

Carol Rudoff is marvellous! Besides her other chores, she is the founder and guiding light of the American Allergy Association. Now she has created a cookbook for making (no laughter, please) hypoallergenic cookies. NO EGGS. NO SOY. NO WHEAT. NO MILK. NO CORN. JUST GOOD TASTE!

How she did this may be a mystery, but allergy patients can now eat and enjoy. So BON APPETITE and all hail the brilliant Carol. This is one time when the allergic children won't toss their cookies.

KIDS (Not for Mommy to read.)

You, too, can be a cookie monster. Make cookies better than Granny's, because you can really eat these. Sure you can do it. Get out your Easy Bake oven and have a go at it.

Take it from me, your friendly allergist, that these cookies will not make you sneeze, wheeze, or itch. Carol's cookies will make even *your* fussy taste buds smile. So eat today—you have nothing to lose but your waistline.

Donald L. Unger, M.D.
formerly Chief of the Allergy Department,
Stritch School of Medicine (Loyola)
now in practice in California

𝒫reface

Sometimes it seems that the only word in your child's vocabulary is "cookie." If your child has a second word, that word is "more."

Keeping up with children's demands for cookies is no easy job and if your children have various food allergies, keeping up may seem insurmountable, as you try to produce cookies appropriate for each child's allergies.

With allergen-free recipes from *The Allergy Cookie Jar,* you can bake cookies for all occasions and still maintain the diet your doctor has prescribed. *The Allergy Cookie Jar* does it for you by eliminating the major food allergens automatically. For gluten-free recipes, use the rice flour substitution table in the Guidelines section, page 3.

When your children want to help, there is no problem. Little ones can mix and stir and taste to their hearts' content. Recipes are free of most common allergens.

When your children want a little more independence in their baking, refer them to the section called *Children's Hour.* Because children with food allergies need to be comfortable taking care of their needs by learning to cook and bake for themselves, these recipes will provide them with the success experiences they need to produce baked products they can be proud of.

So enjoy baking cookies for family and friends, and when your child says, "I want a cookie," smile!

C.D.R.

GUIDELINES

Baking without the standard ingredients called for in most recipes is an adventure. Results are subject to the weather, length of storage of ingredients, and a carefully orchestrated balance among the various ingredients.

INFLUENCES ON BAKING RESULTS

ACCURACY

First check the accuracy of the oven temperature. If you are baking in two ovens, check both since they can differ. Gas ovens require oxygen to burn and pull more air and moisture from the ingredients.

Check the accuracy of your timers. They can be off by a surprising amount. Measure carefully. Solid ingredients should be flattened across the tops of measuring implements. When using a cup to measure liquids, check the liquid level at your eye level.

PAN COLOR AND TIMING

If you have dark-colored baking pans, especially the black finish ones, turn the oven temperature down 25 degrees. For cookies, set the timer for several minutes less than the recipe calls for and check frequently for doneness. Taste the cookies to be sure they have the color and texture (crunchy or chewy) you are looking for. Mark on the recipe your actual baking time for future reference. When baking two sheets in the same oven, the bottom sheet cookies may brown first and may even burn before the top sheet is ready. Be prepared to remove the bottom sheet first or to switch sheet locations halfway through the baking time. You may also want to turn the sheets front to back as the cookies toward the back of the oven tend to brown faster.

WEATHER

Since flours can lose moisture during the winter, there

will be days when your dough may require more liquid and days when your dough may require more flour. These additions depend upon how the ingredients 'go together.' If the batter is obviously dry, add water. If it is too soft to handle, add more flour. Cold and heat also affect creaming margarine and sugar.

INGREDIENTS

MARGARINE

Read margarine labels carefully. Although some diet margarines do not contain milk, they will probably contain corn and/or soy (partially hydrogenated vegetable protein). We have not been able to find a margarine free of milk, corn, and soy. If you are sensitive to all three, and if your doctor approves, you may wish to use butter in your baking rather than margarine. Under these circumstances, Dr. William C. Deamer, late Professor Emeritus of the University of California, permitted the use of butter as it is low in the proteins that usually cause allergy problems and is corn-free and soy-free.

FLOURS

BARLEY

Barley has a good flavor and is a fine, basic flour for baked goods. The recipes in this book are based on barley. If you wish to use other flours, you may experiment using the equivalents recommended below.

RICE FLOUR FOR GLUTEN-FREE BAKING

Rice is grainy and sweet and an excellent flour on which to base recipes; in fact some may taste even better with rice flour; rice and potato starch are a good combination.

Rice flour is gluten free, so use the Barley and Rice Equivalent table to substitue rice flour for barley in these recipes.

WHEAT EQUIVALENTS:

1 cup of wheat flour equals

1 cup rye meal
1 to 1/4 cups rye flour
1 cup potato flour
1 1/3 cups rolled oats
   or oat flour
1/2 cup potato flour plus
   1/2 cup rye flour
5/8 cup potato starch
5/8 cup rice plus
   1/3 cup rye flour

BARLEY AND RICE EQUIVALENTS

BARLEY FLOUR	RICE FLOUR
1 cup is equivalent to	1 cup less 2 tablespoons
1 1/4 cups is equivalent to	1 1/4 cups less 3 1/2 tablespoons
1 1/3 cups	1 1/4 cups plus 1 tablespoon
1 1/2 cups	1 1/3 cups less 2 tablespoons
1 2/3 cups	1 1/2 cups plus 2 1/3 tablespoons
1 3/4 cups	1 1/2 cups
2 cups is equivalent to	1 3/4 cups
2 1/4 cups	2 cups
2 1/3 cups	2 cups plus 2 1/2 teaspoons
2 1/2 cups	2 1/4 cups less 1 tablespoon
3 cups is equivalent to	2 2/3 cups less 1 tablespoon

INGREDIENTS

EGGS

The egg substitute used in these recipes was Jolly Joan Egg Replacer by Ener-G Foods, Inc. Egg substitutes such as **Eggbeaters** or **Scramblers** eliminate **only** egg yolk (cholesterol). They contain egg whites, casein and milk and are **not** suitable.

SUGARS

Turbinado is a partially refined, coarse brown sugar with a molasses flavor. Brown sugar is made from sugar cane or beets and has molasses added for a brown shade.

Granulated sugar is derived from either beets or cane and is 99.5% sucrose. Some sugars now available are a combination of sucrose with dextrose added in order to attract moisture to the baked product.

Liquid sugars have different sweetening abilities and a higher moisture content than non-liquid sugars; they, therefore, increase the moisture content of the baked product.

Confectioner's or powdered sugar has a small amount of cornstarch added in order to lessen lumping. If you are very corn sensitive, do not use this sugar. Do not substitute for granulated sugar in baking.

Honey is another sugar and is recognized and digested by the body as a sugar. It contains two sugars: levulose and dextrose. Some honeys may have glucose added. Honey is sweeter than sugar and is semi-liquid, so using it in a recipe calls for some changes. Warming honey in some hot water before measuring it makes it easier to measure. Cookies made with honey will have a little coarser texture and will be moist and soft.

Honey substitution formulas are:

1. Decrease the amount of sugar by half and use honey in that amount minus 1 tablespoon of liquid less per cup called for in the recipe.

2. Decrease water in the recipe by 1/2 cup for each cup of honey used.

3. For each cup of honey you add, consider it equal to 1 1/4 cups of sugar and decrease the liquid by 1/4 cup and add an extra pinch of baking soda.

4. For every 1/3 cup of white sugar or every 1/2 cup of brown sugar you wish to substitute for, use an extra 1/2 cup flour, 3/4 cup honey and 1/2 teaspoon baking soda

With so many honey substitution formulas available, it is clear that your choice depends on your taste.

CAROB

Carob is a sweet, high protein, low fat bean, the same color as cocoa with an interesting flavor that is enjoyable in its own right. It is caffeine free and not expensive. With the approval of your doctor, it makes an excellent substitute for chocolate.

Carob powder is available in most health food stores and can be used on an equal basis to replace cocoa in a recipe. Oven temperature should be lowered 25 degrees before baking. If you decide to *add* carob rather than use it as a substitute, remember that it is sweeter than sugar.

If you are unable to find carob chips without milk products, use the following method:

Sift 1 cup of carob powder and add 1 cup of water. Blend, boil and then stir over low heat. Cool until syrup is smooth. (Syrup may be stored, uncovered, in the refrigerator.) Spread the syrup thinly on a paper plate and freeze it. You can then break the frozen carob into chips for use in carob chip cookies.

BAKING POWDER

There are three basic kinds of baking powders. Tartrate baking powders are quick in reaction and should not be refrigerated or frozen first. Phosphate baking powders are slower and most active in cold dough. Double-acting baking powders start to work in cold dough, but provide most of their leavening power in the oven. Read the labels before using.

The recipes in this book have been tested using Featherweight Baking Powder, cereal-free and available in health food stores. It is manufactured by Chicago Dietetic Supply, Inc.

To substitute for 1 teaspoon of baking powder, try 1/2 teaspoon cream of tartar and 1/2 teaspoon baking soda.

Another method is to combine 2 teaspoons cream of tartar, 1 teaspoon bicarbonate of soda, and 1/2 teaspoon salt. Use this for each cup of flour. If you are using flours other than wheat, use 2 1/2 times as much per cup.

The carbon dioxide in baking powder has more leavening action at high altitudes. Use less baking powder.

SPECIFICALLY COOKIES

GREASING COOKIE SHEETS

If you have difficulty finding a suitable shortening to grease cookie sheets with, try placing cookies on sheets of aluminum foil. They will keep your cookies from sticking and save you wash up time. You can clean the foil with paper toweling and use it again.

Only some recipes specifically call for using foil on cookie sheets. Please use foil where it is called for. When it is not specifically called for, you may use either foil or grease the sheets.

WATER

Where I have used water in the recipes (not the water with the egg substitute), you may want to experiment by substituting with fruit juices: orange, apple, pineapple, apricot or grape for flavor variation and for added nutrition.

COOLING RACKS

Cooling racks should raise cookies at least 1 1/2 inches above the counter so they won't get soggy. A full two inches is better if the cookies are large.

FRUITS

If using dried currants, dates, figs, or raisins, they must be fresh because baking won't soften them. You can soften currants or rains in boiling water; drain and dry them.

STORAGE

You may rarely have storage problems, but if you've baked several batches of cookies, you may. To store at room temperature, keep covered in an air tight container; be sure that soft cookies are not in the same container as crisp cookies.

For longer storage, place in plastic freezer boxes, date and freeze. They will hold for about two to three months. Thaw frozen cookies in the container at room temperature.

JAMS

For jams without corn syrup, try Scarborough (sugar, fruit, lemon juice, and fruit pectin) or Samodan (fruit, sugar, rum, citric acid, and pectin).

CHILDREN'S SECTION

The recipes in the children's section have been chosen for their ease in preparation. They are not meant, however, for little ones to make on their own. Please be available for questions and for more difficult procedures such as picking up a bowl and pouring the contents into another bowl, putting pans in the oven and taking them out, and, especially, when dough needs slicing. You may also want to demonstrate how to measure solids and liquids accurately.

Always read labels. Ingredients change.

Drop Cookies

SPICY PUMPKIN DROPS

61 cookies
375° oven
10-12 minutes

3/4 cup milk-free margarine
2/3 cup brown sugar, packed
2 teaspoons egg substitute, plus 4 tablespoons water
1 1/2 teaspoons vanilla extract
1 cup canned or cooked fresh pumpkin
2 cups barley flour
5 teaspoons cereal-free baking powder
1/2 teaspoon baking soda
1 1/2 teaspoons ground cinnamon
1/2 teaspoon ground nutmeg
1/4 teaspoon ground cloves
   pinch of ground ginger
1 cup raisins

     In a large bowl, beat together the margarine, sugar, egg substitute and water, and vanilla until light and fluffy. Beat in pumpkin. Add the flour together with the spices, beating until blended. Stir in raisins. With a teaspoon, drop 2 inches apart on an ungreased cookie sheet and bake. Cool on a rack.

VARIATION: PUMPKIN DROPS WITH DATES: Substitute 1 cup of pitted dates, chopped, for the 1 cup of raisins.

VARIATION: PUMPKIN DROPS WITH PRUNES: Substitue 1 cup of chopped, pitted prunes for the 1 cup of raisins.

BANANA DROPS

40 cookies
350° oven
12-14 minutes

3/4 cup milk-free margarine
3/4 cup brown sugar, packed
2 teaspoons egg substitute, plus 4 tablespoons water
1 teaspoon vanilla extract
1 cup mashed bananas, about 3 bananas
1 1/2 teaspoons ground cinnamon
1/2 teaspoon ground nutmeg
2 1/4 cups barley flour
5 5/8 teaspoons cereal-free baking powder
1/4 teaspoon baking soda
1/2 cup raisins, optional

Smooth cake-like cookies that are nutritious, too

Beat together the margarine, sugar, egg substitute and water, and vanilla until light and fluffy. Beat in the bananas, the cinnamon and nutmeg. Add the flour, baking powder and baking soda to the margarine mixture and beat until blended. Stir in the raisins. The dough will be sticky. Drop by the rounded teaspoonful, 2 inches apart, on greased or foil covered sheets and bake until golden. Cool on racks.

TANGY SOFTIES

36 cookies
375° oven
10-12 minutes

1/4 cup milk-free margarine
3/4 cup brown sugar, packed
1 teaspoon egg substitute, plus 2 tablespoons water
1 teaspoon vanilla
1 tablespoon grated orange peel
   pinch of salt
1 1/2 cups barley flour
1/2 teaspoon baking soda
3/4 cup chopped, fresh cranberries

   Beat together the margarine, sugar, egg substitute and water, vanilla, grated orange peel and salt until light and fluffy. Add the flour and soda to the margarine mixture and beat until well blended. Carefully fold in cranberries. Drop by the rounded teaspoonful, 2 inches apart, on greased cookie sheets and bake until golden. Cool on racks.

APPLESAUCE N' CAROB COOKIES

22 cookies
350° oven
25 minutes

2 1/2 cups barley flour
1 teaspoon baking soda
1/2 teaspoon salt
1 1/2 teaspoons cinnamon
1/2 teaspoon powdered cloves
1 teaspoon instant coffee, not crystals
2 tablespoons boiling water
1 (1/4 lb.) stick milk-free margarine
1 cup sugar
1 teaspoon egg substitute, plus 2 tablespoons water
1/4 cup powdered carob
1 1/2 cups smooth applesauce (commercial applesauce may
   contain corn syrup, so use homemade applesauce)
1 cup raisins

     Stir together the flour, soda, salt, cinnamon and cloves. Dissolve the coffee in the boiling water. Cream the margarine in a large bowl and then add sugar, mixing well. Add the egg substitute and water and beat again. Beat in the carob, the coffee, and the applesauce. Add the flour mixture to the carob-applesauce mixture, beating only until mixed. Stir in raisins. Using a 1/4 cup measuring cup for each cookie, place 5 cookies on a foil-covered cookie sheet and bake. Cool on racks that are raised well off counter level. While cookies are cooling, make icing.

CAROB ICING: Place 1 1/2 cups sifted confectioner's sugar, 1/2 cup powdered carob, and a pinch of salt into a mixing bowl. Melt 5 1/3 tablespoons milk-free margarine and pour it, along with 3 tablespoons boiling water, into the mixing bowl. Beat until smooth. The icing should be thick enough not to run. Adjust the consistency with water or sugar. Spoon the icing onto each cookie and spread. Let set for a few hours.

ZUCCHINI COOKIES

55 cookies
350º oven
10-12 minutes

1 cup milk-free margarine
1 cup brown sugar, packed
1 teaspoon egg substitute, plus 2 tablespoons water
1 1/2 teaspoons vanilla
1 cup grated, unpeeled, raw zucchini
2 to 2 1/4 cups barley flour
5 teaspoons cereal-free baking powder
1 teaspoon baking soda
1 1/2 teaspoons ground cinnamon
1 1/2 teaspoons ground nutmeg
  pinch of salt

Have a garden bonanza of zucchini? Now's the perfect time for zucchini cookies and zucchini cookies and zucchini cookies.

Beat together the margarine, sugar, egg substitute and water, and vanilla until light and fluffy. Stir in zucchini. Add 2 cups of flour, baking powder, soda, spices and salt, beating until well blended. Depending upon the wetness of the zucchini, you may need to add more flour. Drop by the teaspoonful on an ungreased baking sheet, 2 inches apart, and bake until lightly browned. Cool on racks.

JACK O' SPICE COOKIES

48 cookies
375° oven
18 minutes

2 1/2 cups sifted flour
6 1/4 teaspoons cereal-free baking powder
1/2 teaspoon salt
1 teaspoon ground cinnamon
3/4 teaspoon ground nutmeg
1/2 teaspoon ground ginger
1/4 teaspoon powdered cloves
1/4 teaspoon allspice
1 (1/4 lb.) stick of milk-free margarine
1 cup sugar
1/2 cup brown sugar, packed
2 teaspoons egg substitute, plus 4 tablespoons water
1 3/4 (1 lb. can) cups canned pumpkin
1 cup raisins

These are delicious, spicy, old-fashioned cookies.

Stir together the flour, baking powder, and all spices. In a separate bowl, cream the margarine. Beat in the sugar and the brown sugar. Add 1 teaspoon of egg substitute along with 2 tablespoons of water and beat. Add the second teaspoon of egg substitute along with 2 tablespoons of water and beat. Beat in the pumpkin. Take the flour mixture and blend into margarine and sugar mixture only until mixed. Stir in the raisins. Drop by the rounded tablespoonful 1 to 1 1/2-inches apart on cookie sheets lined with aluminum foil and bake. While the cookies are baking, prepare glaze. When the cookies are done, slide the foil off the sheet and immediately brush the glaze generously over the tops. Cool on racks.

LEMON GLAZE: Beat together until smooth 2 tablespoons soft, milk-free margarine, 1 1/2 cups confectioner's sugar, a pinch of salt, 2 tablespoons lemon juice, and 1 tablespoon water.

MOLASSES SPICE COOKIES

36 cookies
350° oven
12-13 minutes

2 1/4 cups barley flour
2 teaspoons baking soda
2 teaspoons ground ginger
1 teaspoon ground cinnamon
1/4 teaspoon powdered cloves
1/4 teaspoon salt
2 teaspoons instant coffee, not crystals
1/3 cup boiling water
1 (1/4 lb.) stick milk-free margarine
1/2 cup sugar
1 teaspoon egg substitute, plus 2 tablespoons water
1/2 cup molasses
1 tablespoon whole aniseed

Stir together the flour, baking soda, ginger, cinnamon, cloves and salt. Dissolve the instant coffee in the boiling water. Cream the margarine and beat in the sugar and egg substitute and water. Beat in the molasses. Blend in one half of the dry ingredients. Beat in the coffee and then beat in the remaining dry ingredients. Stir in the aniseed. Drop by the heaping teaspoonful 2 inches apart on aluminum foil-covered cookie sheets and bake. Cool on racks. While the cookies are cooling, prepare the icing.

VANILLA ICING: Combine 3 cups sifted confectioner's sugar with 1 1/2 teaspoons vanilla and 5 tablespoons water. Stir until smooth. The icing should not be so thin that it runs off the cookie. Adjust the consistency by adding sugar or water. Spread on cookies and let set.

DATE COOKIES

35 cookies
350° oven
15 minutes

1 cup pitted dates cut into medium-size pieces
2 cups barley flour
1 teaspoon baking soda
1 teaspoon cream of tartar
1/2 teaspoon ground cinnamon
2 sticks (1/2 lb.) milk-free margarine
1 teaspoon vanilla
1/2 cup sugar
1 cup brown sugar, packed
2 teaspoons egg substitute, plus 4 tablespoons water

Date cookies are a crisp, yet chewy, old-fashioned wafer. If allowed, you may fold in 1 cup of walnuts, broken into medium-size pieces, along with the dates. Store in an air-tight container to keep edges crisp.

Place dates in a mixing bowl and toss them with about 2 tablespoons of the barley flour to coat. Stir together the remaining flour, soda, cream of tartar, and cinnamon. In a separate bowl, cream the margarine and then beat in the vanilla and both sugars. Add 1 teaspoon egg substitute and 2 tablespoons of water and beat. Add the second teaspoon and 2 tablespoons water and beat again. Gradually blend in the dry ingredients. Stir in the dates. Drop dough by the heaping teaspoonful, 3 inches apart, 5 to a sheet, on aluminum foil-covered cookie sheets. Slightly flatten each cookie with the back of a spoon and bake. After baking, let stand a few seconds and then remove to a rack to cool.

MORNING COOKIES

30 cookies
350° oven
10-12 minutes

1/2 cup milk-free margarine
1/2 cup sugar
1 teaspoon egg substitute, plus 2 tablespoons water
2 tablespoons thawed, frozen orange-juice concentrate
1 tablespoon grated orange peel
1 1/4 cups barley flour
2 1/2 teaspoons cereal-free baking powder
1/2 lb. bacon, cooked crisp, drained and crumbled
1/2 cup crisp, rice cereal

No excuse for skipping breakfast with these cookies to tempt the most sleepy appetite.

Beat together the margarine, sugar, egg substitute and water, the orange juice concentrate, and the orange peel. Add the flour and baking powder; beat until well blended. Stir in the bacon and the cereal and drop by the teaspoonful, 2 inches apart, on ungreased cookie sheets. Bake until the edges are golden. Cool on racks and store in the refirgerator.

MOLASSES CHEWS

36 cookies
375° oven
10 minutes

1 1/4 sticks of milk-free margarine
1 cup brown sugar, packed
1/4 cup molasses
2 1/2 cups barley flour
1 teaspoon baking soda
1/4 teaspoon mace
  pinch of salt
1 teaspoon egg substitute, plus 2 tablespoons water
1/2 teaspoon vanilla extract

Crisp, yet chewy and perfect for your cookie jar.

Melt the margarine in a saucepan over moderate heat. Add the sugar and molasses, stirring until the sugar is melted. Bring to a rolling boil then remove from the heat and set aside to cool. Meanwhile, stir together the flour, baking soda, mace and salt. Add the egg substitute and water and vanilla to the cooled margarine mixture, beating until smooth. Blend in the dry ingredients. Drop by the rounded teaspoonful 1 1/2 inches apart on aluminum foil-covered cookie sheets and bake. Cool on racks.

CAROB BANANA COOKIES

55 cookies
400° oven
12-14 minutes

1 cup carob chips
2 1/4 cups barley flour
5 3/4 teaspoons cereal-free baking powder
1/4 teaspoon baking soda
1/2 teaspoon salt
1 stick plus 2 2/3 tablespoons milk-free margarine
1/2 teaspoon vanilla extract
1 cup sugar
2 teaspoons egg substitute, plus 4 tablespoons water
1 cup mashed bananas, about 2 large bananas

These giant cookies will have your family begging for more.

Place carob chips in a double boiler over hot water. Cover and cook until partially melted, then uncover and stir until completely melted and smooth. Set aside to cool. Stir together the flour, baking powder, soda and salt and set aside. Cream the margarine; add vanilla and sugar and beat well. Add 1 teaspoon egg substitute and 2 tablespoons of water and beat. Add the second teaspoon of egg substitute and 2 tablespoons of water and beat. On low speed, gradually add half the flour, beating only until mixed. Add the carob and banana, beating until smooth. Add the remaining flour, beating only until smooth. Drop the cookies by the heaping teaspoonful 2 inches apart on an aluminum foil-covered baking sheet and bake. Let stand 1 minute after baking and then transfer to racks to cool.

APPLE-RAISIN DROPS

54 cookies
350° oven
12-14 minutes

1/2 cup milk-free margarine, softened
1 cup brown sugar, packed
2 teaspoons egg substitute, plus 4 tablespoons water
1/4 cup water
2 cups barley flour
5 teaspoons cereal-free baking powder
1 teaspoon ground cinnamon
1/2 teaspoon salt
1/2 teaspoon ground nutmeg
1/4 teaspoon ground cloves
2 medium apples, peeled, cored, and chopped
1 cup raisins

Set the apples aside until you need them in bowl full of water with a few drops of lemon to prevent the apples from turning brown.

Cream the margarine and sugar. Add the egg substitute and water and the 1/4 cup water, beating well. Stir the flour together with the spices and then stir into the creamed mixture. Stir in apples and raisins. Drop on a well-greased cookie sheet and bake. Cool on a rack.

Refrigerator Cookies

LEMON-ANISE COOKIES

42 cookies
400° oven
10 minutes

1 3/4 cups barley flour
1/4 teaspoon salt
4 1/2 teaspoons cereal-free baking powder
1 (1/4 lb.) stick milk-free margarine
1/2 teaspoon vanilla
1 cup sugar
1 teaspoon egg substitute, plus 2 tablespoons water
1 teaspoon aniseed
  grated rind of 1 lemon

You'll love these golden-yellow cookies with their golden-yellow flecks. They have a fresh lemon taste and a fragrance that will linger.

Stir together the flour, salt and baking powder. Cream the margarine and then beat in the vanilla and sugar. Add the egg substitute and water and aniseed. Gradually, mix in the dry ingredients. Stir in the lemon rind. Tear off a 15-inch piece of wax paper. Place the dough by large spoonsful, lengthwise, down the middle of the paper for 10 inches. Fold the paper up on the long side. Press against dough through the paper to form a roll about 11 inches long, 1 inch thick. Freeze until firm. Cut dough into 1/4-inch slices. Place 1 inch apart on foil-lined cookie sheets and bake. Cool on racks.

ABERDEEN CRISPS

50 cookies
400° oven
10 minutes

2 2/3 cups barley flour
1/2 teaspoon baking soda
1/8 teaspoon salt
  grated rind of 1 lemon
2 tablespoons lemon juice
1 (1/4 lb.) stick milk-free margarine
1 cup sugar
1 teaspoon egg substitute, plus 2 tablespoons water
2 teaspoons caraway seeds

These aromatic cookies may be stored for months in the freezer before baking.

Stir together the flour, soda, and salt. Combine the lemon rind and juice. Cream the margarine, beating in sugar, egg substitute and water, and seeds. Mix dry ingredients in and then lemon rind and lemon juice mixture. Knead the dough with your hands until mixture holds together and is smooth. Form the dough into a roll 10 inches long and 2 inches in diameter. Wrap in wax paper and freeze several hours or longer. Slice the cookies 1/4 inch thick and place them on ungreased sheets 1 inch apart. Bake and cool on racks.

LEMON DELIGHT

48 cookies
375° oven
10-12 minutes

1 cup milk-free margarine
1 cup sugar
1 teaspoon egg substitute, plus 2 tablespoons water
1 1/2 teaspoons grated lemon peel
1 tablespoon lemon juice
1 tablespoon water
2 3/4 cups barley flour
1/4 teaspoon baking soda
1/4 teaspoon salt
1/3 cup grated carob chips (whirl them in the food processor)

These cookies have an absolutely delicious, delicate lemon flavor and fragrance. Try them with a light tea like jasmine.

Cream together the margarine and sugar. Beat in the egg substitute and water, peel, lemon juice, and water. In a second bowl, stir together the flour, soda and salt and combine with the creamed mixture. Stir in the grated carob. Shape dough into 2 9-inch rolls. Wrap in wax paper or clear plastic wrap. Chill thoroughly—about 3 hours. Cut into 1/4-inch slices and place on ungreased cookie sheets. Bake and cool on racks.

SOUTHERN SESAME

48 cookies
375° oven
15 minutes

3/4 cup sesame seeds
1 (1/4 lb.) stick milk-free margarine
3/4 teaspoon vanilla
1/8 teaspoon salt
1 cup sugar
1 teaspoon egg substitute, plus 2 tablespoons water
2 cups barley flour
1/4 cup water

In a large, heavy frying pan, over medium-low heat, constantly stir sesame seeds and shake the pan until the seeds are a golden brown. Transfer the seeds to a plate and let them cool. Cream the margarine. Add the vanilla, salt, and sugar, beating until blended. Add the egg substitute and water and beat to mix. Keep beating at low speed and add half the flour, all the water, and then the rest of the flour. Beat only until smooth. Mix in the sesame seeds. If the dough is too soft to handle, chill it. With a tablespoon, place dough lengthwise down the center of a strip of 18-inch long wax paper. Press the dough into an oblong 12 inches long and about 1 inch thick. Freeze overnight. Place the dough on a barley-floured work surface and cut into 1/4-inch slices. Place 1 inch apart on foil-wrapped cookie sheets and bake. Cool on racks.

PINWHEEL COOKIES

40 cookies
350° oven
12 minutes

1 3/4 cups barley flour
4 1/2 teaspoons cereal-free baking powder
1/4 teaspoon salt
3 tablespoons carob powder, plus 1 tablespoon water
1 (1/4 lb.) stick milk-free margarine
3/4 cup sugar
1 teaspoon egg substitute, plus 2 tablespoons water
1 teaspoon instant coffee, not crystals
1/4 teaspoon almond extract

Enjoy the ooh's and aah's when these cookies make their appearance—you deserve them.

Stir together the flour, baking powder and salt. In a double boiler on moderate heat and over hot water, stir the carob powder and water and set aside to cool. Cream the margarine. Add vanilla and sugar, beating to mix. Add the egg substitute and water and beat well. Slowly, blend in the flour mixture. Divide the dough in half. To one half the dough, add the melted carob and the coffee powder; mix. To the other half, add almond extract; mix. Tear off 4 pieces of wax paper, each about 17 inches long. On one piece, place the almond dough. Cover with another piece. Flatten the dough with your hands. With a rolling pin, roll over the paper to roll the the dough into an oblong 9x14 inches. Try to keep the edges the same thickness. Repeat with the second half of the dough. Freeze the doughs for 10 minutes. Remove top piece of wax paper from both doughs. Place the carob dough over the white dough. (Be careful; you must get it right the first time.) Remove the paper from the carob roll. (If paper is difficult to remove, reverse doughs with carob on bottom and remove paper from the almond dough or freeze another 5 minutes. Let warm before attempting to roll.) Using the paper under the white dough, roll the doughs with your hands in jelly-roll fashion, starting with the long side. Wrap the roll in wax paper and freeze until firm. Cut firm dough into 1/4-inch slices and place 1 inch apart on ungreased cookie sheets. Bake and cool on racks.

BUTTERSCOTCH COOKIES

70 cookies
375° oven
8-10 minutes

2 cups barley flour
1/2 teaspoon baking soda
1/2 teaspoon cream of tartar
1/8 teaspoon salt
1 (1/4 lb.) stick milk-free margarine
1/2 teaspoon vanilla extract
1 cup brown sugar, packed
1 teaspoon egg substitute, plus 2 tablespoons water

Stir together the flour, soda, cream of tartar, and salt. Cream the margarine then add vanilla and sugar, beating well. Add the egg substitute and water and beat until smooth. Add the dry ingredients to the creamed ingredients, beating until the mixture is firm. With your hands, form dough into a long rectangle on wax paper. Fold the paper over the dough and press and smooth the dough to form a 12- to 14-inch long roll about 2 inches in diameter. Place dough in the freezer for several hours or overnight. Cut dough into 1/4-inch slices and bake 1 inch apart on foil-covered cookie sheets. Cool on racks.

OLDE FASHIONED ICEBOX COOKIES

45 cookies
350° oven
18-20 minutes

2 (1/2 lb.) sticks milk-free margarine
1 teaspoon nutmeg
2 cups sugar
2 teaspoons egg substitute, plus 4 tablespoons water
3 cups barley flour
  grated rind of 1 lemon

Cream the margarine; add nutmeg and sugar, beating well. Add 1 teaspoon egg substitute, and 2 tablespoons water and beat well. Add the second teaspoon egg substitute and water and beat well. Blend in flour until smooth and blend in the rind. Divide dough. Shape each half into a long roll on wax paper. Flour your hands with barley flour if needed to keep dough from sticking. Wrap the rolls in wax paper and freeze for several hours or overnight. Unwrap dough and cut into 1/4-inch slices and place 1 inch apart on foil-wrapped sheets. Bake and cool on racks.

TEA TIME

80 cookies
375º oven
8-10 minutes

1 cup milk-free margarine
2 cups brown sugar, packed
2 teaspoons egg substitute, plus 4 tablespoons water
2 tablespoons vanilla
3 1/2 cups barley flour
8 3/4 teaspoons cereal-free baking powder
  granulated sugar, optional

Great for lemonade time, too.

Beat together the margarine, sugar, egg substitute and water, and vanilla until light and fluffy. Add flour and baking powder, beating until blended. Dough will be stiff. Divide the dough into 4 equal parts and shape each into a 7-inch log. Wrap and refrigerate until firm, several hours or overnight. Lightly grease cookie sheets and cut the dough into 1/4-inch slices. Sprinkle with sugar, if you wish. Bake until golden; if you like a crunchier cookie, bake little longer. Cool on racks.

SURPRISE PILLOWS

36 cookies
350° oven
12 minutes

1 1/2 cups brown sugar, packed
1/2 cup milk-free margarine
1 teaspoon egg substitute, plus 2 tablespoons water
3/4 teaspoon vanilla
2 1/2 cups barley flour
1 1/2 teaspoons cream of tartar
1 1/2 teaspoons baking soda
1 1/2 teaspoons vinegar
1/2 cup water
　　date filling (recipe below)

You can store these cookies in an airtight container for up to 1 week or mix them a day ahead.

Cream together the sugar, margarine, egg substitute and water, and vanilla. Combine the flour, cream of tartar, and soda. Stir the vinegar with the water. Add the vinegar mixture to the creamed mixture alternately with the flour mixture, mixing until blended. Cover and chill for 8 hours. Roll out the dough, a portion at a time, on a heavily barley-floured board. Use a barley-floured, 2-inch, plain cookie cutter. Place half of the cookies 2 inches apart on greased baking sheets. Top each with 2 teaspoons date filling and cover with a second cookie. Press the edges with the back of the tines of a fork to seal. Bake until brown and cool on racks.

DATE FILLING: Gently boil and stir 3/4 cup orange juice, 1/2 cup sugar and 2 cups chopped, pitted dates for 5 minutes. If permitted, add 1/2 cup chopped nuts and let cool.

CARDAMOM COOKIES

40 cookies
350° oven
15 minutes

2 cups barley flour
1/4 teaspoon baking soda
1 1/2 teaspoons ground cardamom
1 (1/4 lb.) stick milk-free margarine
1 teaspoon vanilla
1/2 cup brown sugar, packed
1/3 cup coconut milk

These cookies puff up nicely; they can be crunchy or soft, depending upon how thickly you slice them. They are a good cookie for a strong tea as they have a mild flavor.

Stir together the flour, soda, and cardamom. Cream the margarine and then beat in the vanilla and sugar. On low speed, add the dry ingredients in three additions, alternating with the coconut milk in two additions. Turn dough out onto a piece of wax paper and knead slightly. Form into an oblong 2 inches wide and 10 inches long. Wrap in wax paper and then freeze for several hours. Slice dough into 1/4-inch slices and place them 1 inch apart on ungreased, foil-lined sheets. Bake and then cool on racks.

Shaped Cookies

SNOWBALLS

60 cookies
350° oven
8 minutes

2 cups barley flour
5 teaspoons cereal-free baking powder
  dash salt
1/4 teaspoon baking soda
3/4 cup milk-free margarine
3/4 cup brown sugar
6 tablespoons carob powder, plus 2 tablespoons water
1 teaspoon egg substitute, plus 2 tablespoons water
1 1/4 teaspoons vanilla
1/4 cup water
  confectioner's sugar

Make these a day ahead. You can bake them just before the children arrive and let them help you roll them in confectioner's sugar.

Stir together the flour, baking powder, salt and soda. Beat together the margarine and sugar until fluffy. Mix the carob powder and water and beat into the margarine mixture. Beat in the egg substitute and water, the vanilla, and the water. Add the dry ingredients, a little at a time, blending to make a stiff dough. Chill overnight or until firm enough to handle. Using your hands, roll the dough, a teaspoonful at a time, to make marble-size balls and place them about 2 inches apart on cookie sheets. Bake and remove them carefully from the sheets. Roll in confectioner's sugar while they are still hot. Cool on racks and then roll again in confectioner's sugar, if you wish.

COCONUT RICE COOKIES

42 cookies
350° oven
10 minutes

1/2 cup milk-free margarine
1/2 cup brown sugar
1/2 cup sugar
1 teaspoon egg substitute, plus 2 tablespoons water
1 teaspoon vanilla
1 1/4 cups barley flour
3 1/4 teaspoons cereal-free baking powder
1/2 teaspoon baking soda
   dash salt
2 cups crisp rice cereal
1 1/3 cups shredded coconut
1 cup dates, chopped and pitted

Cream together margarine with both sugars. Add the egg substitute and water and vanilla, beating well. Stir together the flour, baking powder, soda, and salt and blend with the creamed mixture. Stir in the cereal, coconut, and dates. Form into 3/4-inch balls and place 2 1/2 inches apart on ungreased cookie sheets. Bake and cool slightly on sheets. Cool on racks.

BUTTER COOKIES

30 cookies
300º oven
10-12 minutes

1 cup milk-free margarine
1 cup confectioner's sugar, sifted
1 teaspoon egg substitute, plus 2 tablespoons water, beaten
1 teaspoon vanilla
1/2 teaspoon cream of tartar
1/2 teaspoon baking soda
    pinch salt
2 cups barley flour
    granulated sugar

Cream together the margarine and sugar. Add the egg substitute and water and vanilla. Stir together the cream of tartar, soda, salt and flour and add to the creamed mixture; mix well. Refrigerate until chilled. Roll by hand into small 1-inch diameter balls and place on ungreased cookie sheets. Dip the bottom of a glass into granulated sugar and press the ball to flatten slightly. Bake; let sit 2 minutes before removing from cookie sheet to racks for cooling.

GINGERY SNAPS

40 cookies
375° oven
10-12 minutes

1 cup brown sugar
3/4 cup safflower oil
1/4 cup dark molasses
1 teaspoon egg substitute, plus 2 tablespoons water
2 cups barley flour
2 teaspoons baking soda
1 teaspoon ground cinnamon
1 teaspoon ground ginger
1/2 teaspoon ground cloves
1/4 teaspoon salt
   granulated sugar

Combine the sugar, oil, molasses, egg substitute and water, beating well. Stir together the remaining ingredients, but not the granulated sugar. Gradually blend flour mixture into the molasses mixture. Using about 1 tablespoon for each, form dough into 1 1/4-inch balls. Roll in granulated sugar. Place 2 inches apart on greased cookie sheets and bake. Cool on racks.

MOCHA FINGERS

60 cookies
375° oven
10-12 minutes

1 cup milk-free margarine
3/4 cup sugar
1 teaspoon egg substitute, plus 2 tablespoons water
1 teaspoon vanilla
2 1/4 cups barley flour
2 tablespoons instant coffee crystals
5 teaspoons cereal-free baking powder
  dash salt

Cream together the margarine and sugar. Beat in the egg substitute and water and vanilla. Stir together the flour, coffee, baking powder and salt and slowly blend into the creamed mixture. Use the star plate and force the dough through a cookie press into 3-inch strips on an ungreased sheet. Bake; cool on racks. Dip one end of each cookie into Carob Glaze.

CAROB GLAZE: Melt 3 tablespoons powdered carob, 1 tablespoon water, and 1 tablespoon milk-free margarine over hot water in a double boiler. Stir in 3 1/2 tablespoons water. Add 1 cup sifted confectioner's sugar and stir until smooth. Adjust consistency with water or sugar. You are aiming towards a cream-like consistency, but not so heavy that the glaze does not adhere to the cookie without breaking it. If you have difficulty dipping, spread the glaze on.

CRACKLE COOKIES

34 cookies
350° oven
12-14 minutes

2/3 cup safflower oil
1 cup sugar
1 teaspoon egg substitute, plus 2 tablespoons water
1/4 cup molasses
2 to 2 1/4 cups barley flour
2 teaspoons baking soda
1 teaspoon ground cinnamon
1 teaspoon ground ginger
  granulated sugar

      Combine the oil and sugar. Add the egg substitute and water, beating well. Stir in the molasses, 2 cups of flour, the soda, cinnamon and ginger. You may need to add a little more flour to make a firm dough. Shape dough into 1 1/4-inch balls. Roll in the granulated sugar. Place 3 inches apart on ungreased baking sheets and bake until golden brown and tops crinkle. Cool on racks.

CINNAMON FAVORITES

60 cookies
375° oven
10 minutes

1 cup milk-free margarine
1 1/3 cups sugar
2 teaspoons egg substitute, plus 2 tablespoons water
3 cups barley flour
1 1/2 teaspoons cream of tartar
1 teaspoon baking soda
    pinch salt
    sugar-cinnamon coating

These are sure to become favorites in your family.

Cream the margarine, sugar and egg substitute and water until light and fluffy. Add the remaining ingredients, mixing until blended. Shape into 1-inch balls. Roll the balls in the sugar-cinnamon mixture, covering completely. Place the balls 2 1/2 inches apart on ungreased baking sheets and bake until golden. Cool on racks.

SUGAR-CINNAMON COATING: Mix 2 tablespoons sugar with 1 1/2 teaspoons ground cinnamon.

JAM LOGS

50 cookies
350° oven
15 minutes

3/4 cup milk-free margarine
2/3 cup sugar
1 teaspoon egg substitute, plus 2 tablespoons margarine
1 teaspoon vanilla
2 cups barley flour
5 teaspoons cereal-free baking powder
1/2 teaspoon cinnamon
  jam

Use different jams for each of the dough cylinders.

Cream together the margarine and sugar. Add the egg substitute and vanilla, beating well. Combine flour, baking powder, and cinnamon. Add to creamed mixture in thirds, beating well after each addition. Divide dough into quarters. Roll each quarter into a cylinder, about 12 inches long. Transfer cylinders to baking sheets. Make an indentation about 1/4 inch deep down the center of each cylinder, lengthwise and fill it with jam. Bake until golden. Let cool slightly, then slice the cylinders diagonally into 3/4-inch cookies. Cool on racks.

GINGER SOFTIES

22 cookies
375° oven
13 minutes

2 1/4 cups barley flour
2 teaspoons baking soda
1/2 teaspoon salt
1 1/4 teaspoons ground cinnamon
1 teaspoon ground ginger
1/2 teaspoon powdered cloves
1/4 teaspoon allspice
1 1/2 (3/8 lb.) sticks milk-free margarine
1 cup dark brown sugar, packed
1 teaspoon egg substitute, plus 2 tablespoons water
1/4 cup molasses
  granulated sugar

These are large, dark, and delicious.

Stir together the flour, soda, salt, cinnamon, ginger, cloves, and allspice. Cream the margarine then add the brown sugar, beating well. Add the egg substitute and water and the molasses and beat until the mixture is light in color. On low speed, gradually add the flour mixture. Refrigerate the dough for about 15 minutes or until you can handle it. Using a rounded tablespoonful of dough for each cookie, roll the dough into a ball and then roll the ball in granulated sugar. Place the balls 2 1/2 inches apart on ungreased sheets and bake. Cool on racks.

GINGERY, GINGERY SNAPPERS

22 cookies
375° oven
13 minutes

2 cups plus 2 tablespoons barley flour
2 teaspoons baking soda
  dash salt
1 teaspoon cinnamon
2 teaspoons ginger
1/2 teaspoon powdered cloves
1/4 teaspoon allspice
1/4 teaspoon finely ground black pepper, optional
1 1/2 (3/8 lb.) sticks milk-free margarine
1 cup brown sugar
1 teaspoon egg substitute, plus 2 tablespoons water
1/4 cup molasses
  finely grated rind of 1 lemon
  finely grated rind of 1 orange
  granulated sugar

These large cookies are extra gingery. Be prepared.

Stir together the flour, soda, salt, spices and black pepper, if using. Cream the margarine. Blend in the brown sugar. Add egg substitute and water and molasses, beating until the mixture is light in color. Gradually, blend in the dry ingredients. Stir in the grated rinds. Refrigerate the dough about 30 minutes. Using a rounded tablespoonful of dough for each cookie, roll it into a ball and roll it in the granulated sugar. Place the balls 3 inches apart on an ungreased cookie sheet and bake. Cool on racks.

CINNAMON-SUGAR COOKIES

75 cookies
375° oven
10-12 minutes

1 cup milk-free margarine
2 cups sugar
2 teaspoons egg substitute, plus 4 tablespoons water
1/4 cup water
1 1/4 teaspoons vanilla
3 3/4 cups barley flour
1/2 teaspoon baking soda
1/2 teaspoon cream of tartar
  dash salt
  sugar-cinnamon coating

      Cream together the margarine and sugar until light and fluffy. Add 1 teaspoon egg substitute and 2 tablespoons water and beat well. Add the second teaspoon egg substitute and 2 tablespoons water and beat well. Blend in water and vanilla. Stir together the flour, soda, cream of tartar and salt and then stir into creamed mixture. Form the dough into 1-inch balls. Dip the bottom of a glass in the sugar-cinnamon mixture and slightly flatten balls with the bottom of the glass. Bake and cool on racks.

SUGAR-CINNAMON COATING: Mix 3 tablespoons sugar with 1 3/4 teaspoons ground cinnamon.

RUSSIAN TEA CAKES

38 cookies
350° oven
13-15 minutes

1 cup milk-free margarine
1/2 cup confectioner's sugar
2 teaspoons vanilla
  pinch salt
2 cups barley flour
1/2 teaspoon baking soda
  confectioner's sugar

A rich-tasing cookie, shaped to your liking, any one of three ways.

Beat together the margarine, sugar, vanilla and salt until light and fluffy. Gradually, beat in the flour and soda, blending well. Drop the dough by the teaspoonful, 2 inches apart on an ungreased baking sheet. Or roll the dough into balls. Or you can form the dough into crescents. Bake until the edges are lightly browned. Cool on racks. While cookies are still warm, you can sift confectioner's sugar over the tops.

CAROB CHIPPERS

27 cookies
350° oven
15 minutes

1 cup milk-free margarine
1 cup confectioner's sugar
1 1/4 teaspoons vanilla extract
1/4 teaspoon salt
2 1/4 cups barley flour
1 cup carob chips
   confectioner's sugar, optional

*Can you have too many carob chip cookie recipes?
Each one is your new favorite and these are rich.*

Beat together the margarine, sugar, vanilla and salt until light and fluffy. Add the flour and blend well; the mixture will be stiff. Stir in the carob chips; shape the dough into 1-inch balls. Place balls 2 inches apart on ungreased baking sheets and flatten with the back of the tines of a fork. Bake and cool on racks. While the cookies are still warm, sift confectioner's sugar over the tops, if you like.

SOUTHERN CHEWS

48 cookies
400° oven
10 minutes

3 cups barley flour
1 teaspoon baking soda
1/2 teaspoon cream of tartar
1/4 teaspoon salt
1 1/2 (3/8 lb.) sticks milk-free margarine
3/4 teaspoon vanilla
1/2 teaspoon almond extract
1 cup sugar
1 cup dark brown sugar
2 teaspoons egg substitute, plus 4 tablespoons water

Crisp, yet chewy cookies with a butterscotch flavor.

Stir together the flour, soda, cream of tartar, and salt. Cream the margarine. Add the vanilla and almond extract and then, gradually, add both sugars, beating well. Add the egg substitute and water and beat until well blended. On low speed, gradually combine the flour mixture. Cover cookie sheets with foil. Take a heaping teaspoonful of dough and roll it to form a ball. Place the balls 2 inches apart on the sheets and bake. Cookies will feel soft after baking, but will harden as they cool. Cool on racks.

Bar Cookies

CAFE BRAVO BARS

32 squares
350° oven
25 minutes

1/2 teaspoon cofee powder, not crystals
1/2 cup hot water
1/2 cup milk-free margarine
1/2 cup brown sugar, packed
1/2 cup sugar
2 teaspoons egg substitute, plus 4 tablespoons water, beaten
2 cups barley flour
1/2 teaspoon baking soda
5 teaspoons cereal-free baking powder
1/2 teaspoon ground cinnamon
1/2 teaspoon ground ginger
1/2 teaspoon ground nutmeg
1/4 teaspoon salt

Delicious. These may be gone by day's end.

Dissolve the coffee in the hot water and refrigerate. Cream together the margarine and both sugars until light and fluffy. Beat in 1 teaspoon egg substitute and 2 tablespoons of water. Beat in the second teaspoon egg substitute and water. Stir together the flour, soda, baking powder, spices and salt. Add the flour mixture alternately to the creamed margarine mixture with the cold coffee. Spread over the bottom of a 15½x10½x1-inch pan and bake. While cooling, make Crystal Glaze and spread over. Cool completely and cut into squares.

CRYSTAL GLAZE: Cream 1/4 cup milk-free margarine until light and fluffy. Beat in 2 cups confectioner's sugar, a dash of salt, and 2 tablespoons cold, strong coffee.

CRANBERRY-ORANGE STRIPE

24 squares
350° oven
10 minutes
20 minutes

Cranberry-Orange Filling
3/4 cup brown sugar, packed
2 cups barley flour
3/4 cup milk-free margarine
1 teaspoon egg substitute, plus 2 tablespoons water
1 teaspoon vanilla

This is a flavorful variation of Apricot Stripe bars. Store baked squares in the refrigerator and use within 3 days.

Prepare the Cranberry-Orange Filling (recipe below) and set aside. Combine the sugar and flour. Use a fork or a pastry blender to cut in the margarine until the size of peas. Set aside 1 cup of this crumb mixture. To the remaining crumb mixture, add the egg substitute and water and vanilla. Beat until well blended and the mixture holds together. Press this mixture evenly on the bottom of a greased 13x9x2-inch baking pan. Bake for 10 minutes. Spread this baked crust with Cranberry-Orange Filling and then sprinkle with the reserved 1 cup of crumb mixture, pressing it into the filling. Bake for 20 minutes or until golden brown. Cool in the pan and cut into bars.

CRANBERRY-ORANGE FILLING: In a medium saucepan, combine 3 cups fresh cranberries, 2/3 cup sugar and 3/4 cup orange juice. Bring to a boil. Reduce to medium heat and continue cooking until the cranberry skins have popped (5 minutes or so); stir from time to time. Stir in 2 teaspoons grated orange peel and 2 tablespoons arrowroot mixed with 1/4 cup cold orange juice. Cook until mixture becomes clear, boils, and thickens, stirring constantly. Cool.

APRICOT STRIPE

24 squares
350° oven
10 minutes
20 minutes

  Apricot Filling
3/4 cup brown sugar, packed
2 cups barley flour
3/4 cup milk-free margarine
1 teaspoon egg substitute, plus 2 tablespoons water
1 teaspoon vanilla

The secret is the apricot filling hidden between cookie-like layers.

Prepare the Apricot Filling (recipe below) and set aside. Combine the sugar and flour. Use a fork or a pastry blender to cut in the margarine until the size of peas. Set aside 1 cup of this crumb mixture. To the remaining crumb mixture, add the egg substitute and water and vanilla. Beat until well blended and the mixture holds together. Press this mixture evenly on the bottom of a greased 13x9x2-inch baking pan. Bake for 10 minutes. Spread this baked crust with Apricot Filling and then sprinkle with the reserved 1 cup of crumb mixture, pressing it into the filling. Bake for 20 minutes or until golden brown. Cool in the pan and cut into bars.

APRICOT FILLING: In a medium saucepan, combine 1 (6 oz.) package of dried apricots (or use your own dried apricots), 1 1/4 cups water, and 1/3 cup sugar. Stir occasionally while bringing to a boil. Reduce to medium heat. Cover and simmer 15 to 25 minutes until apricots are tender and mixture looks like a puree, stirring from time to time. Stir in 1 tablespoon lemon juice.

HONEY BARS

32 squares
350° oven
35 minutes

1 1/3 cups barley flour
3 1/2 teaspoons cereal-free baking powder
  pinch salt
3 teaspoons egg substitute, plus 6 tablespoons water
1 cup honey
1 teaspoon vanilla
2 cups pitted dates, coarsely cut
  confectioner's sugar, optional

Stir together the flour, baking powder and salt. Beat the egg substitute and water; beat in honey and vanilla. Blend in the dry ingredients and stir in the dates. Line a 15½x10½x1-inch baking pan with foil and brush with softened margarine. Dust with barley flour. Spread the dough in the pan. Bake. Cool for 3 minutes and invert onto a rack. Remove the pan and foil. Place another rack over and invert again. Cool completely. Cut into bars and, if you like, sprinkle with confectioner's sugar.

BANANA BARS

32 squares
350° oven
25-35 minutes

3/4 cup milk-free margarine
2/3 cup sugar
2/3 cup brown sugar, packed
1 teaspoon egg substitute, plus 2 tablespoons water
1 teaspoon vanilla
1 cup ripe, mashed bananas (about 2 medium size bananas)
2 cups barley flour
5 teaspoons cereal-free baking powder
1/2 teaspoon salt
1 cup carob chips

Cream together the margarine and both sugars until light and fluffy. Add the egg substitute and water and vanilla, beating well. Stir in banana. Stir together the flour, baking powder, and salt and add to the creamed mixture. Beat well. Stir in the carob pieces. Spread in a greased and barley-floured 15½x10½x1-inch baking pan and bake. Check several times for doneness with a toothpick, starting at 20 minutes; you may need longer than the stated time. Cool before cutting into squares.

CAROB BARS

16 squares
350° oven
28 minutes

1 (1/4 lb.) stick milk-free margarine
6 tablespoons carob powder, plus 2 tablespoons water
1 cup sugar
1/2 teaspoon vanilla extract
2 teaspoons egg substitute, plus 4 tablespoons water
1 cup barley flour
  dash salt

These fudgy bars are whipped up in a saucepan.

Prepare an 8x8-inch, square cake pan by lining it with foil. Melt 1 or 2 tablespoons milk-free margarine and brush it over the foil. Place margarine, carob powder and water in a saucepan over low heat, stirring occasionally until margarine is melted and smooth. Let cool for 3 minutes. Add sugar, vanilla, and 1 teaspoon egg substitute, plus 2 tablespoons water, stirring until smooth. Add second teaspoon egg substitute and 2 tablespoons water, stirring until smooth. Add flour and salt and stir until smooth. Spread evenly in prepared pan and bake (for not more than 28 minutes). Cool for 5 minutes and invert on rack. Remove the pan and foil. Cover with rack and invert. Let cool then cut into squares. Store covered.

GOLDEN BARS

24 bars
350° oven
15 minutes
20-25 minutes

1/2 cup confectioner's sugar
2 cups barley flour
1 cup milk-free margarine
4 teaspoons egg substitute, plus 8 tablespoons water
2 cups sugar
5 teaspoons cereal-free baking powder
1/4 teaspoon salt
2 tablespoons grated lemon peel
1/4 cup fresh lemon juice
   confectioner's sugar

These bars can be made the day before and taken on on your picnic without last minute preparation.

Combine the 1/2 cup confectioner's sugar and flour. With a fork or pastry blender, cut the margarine into the sugar mixture until the mixture is crumbly, the size of small peas. Press the mixture evenly onto the bottom of an ungreased 13x9-inch baking pan and bake for 15 minutes. Meanwhile, beat together the egg substitute and water, the sugar, baking powder, salt, lemon peel and lemon juice until fluffy. Pour over the hot crust and bake again for 20 to 25 minutes until no imprint remains when touched lightly in the center. Cool in pan. While still hot, sift confectioner's sugar over the top. Refrigerate 4 hours or overnight before cutting.

LEMON GLAZE BARS

16 squares
350° oven
12-15 minutes
25 minutes

1 cup barley flour
3/4 cup sugar
1/4 teaspoon salt
6 tablespoons milk-free margarine
1 cup brown sugar, packed
2 tablespoons barley flour
2 1/2 teaspoons cereal-free baking powder
1/4 teaspoon salt
2 teaspoons egg substitute, plus 4 tablespoons water,
    slightly beaten
1 1/2 teaspoons vanilla

Stir together the flour, sugar, salt, and margarine until mixture is crumbly. Pat this mixture into an ungreased 9x9x2-inch baking pan and bake for 12 to 15 minutes. Stir together the brown sugar, flour, baking powder, and salt. Blend in the egg substitute and water and vanilla, mixing well. Spread this mixture over the baked layer and bake again for 25 minutes. While still warm, spread with Lemon Glaze II. Cool in pan and cut into bars.

LEMON GLAZE II: Combine 1/2 cup sifted confectioner's sugar, 1 tablespoon of melted milk-free margarine, and 2 teaspoons lemon juice. Beat until smooth.

CAKE-LIKE, NON-BROWNIES

16 squares
350° oven
25-30 minutes

3/4 cup milk-free margarine
1 cup sugar
3 teaspoons egg substitute, plus 6 tablespoons water
6 tablespoons carob powder, plus 2 tablespoons water
1 teaspoon vanilla
1 1/4 cup barley flour
3 1/2 teaspoons cereal-free baking powder
1/4 teaspoon salt
   confectioner's sugar, optional

      Cream together the margarine and sugar, beating in the egg substitute and water, the carob powder and water, and the vanilla. Stir together the flour, baking powder, and salt and blend into the creamed mixture, mixing well. Grease a 9x9x2-inch baking pan and spread the dough. Bake and cool. If you wish, sift confectioner's sugar over the top. Cut into bars.

MOCHA BARS

16 squares
350° oven
30-35 minutes

1/2 cup milk-free margarine
2/3 cup sugar
2 teaspoons egg substitute, plus 2 tablespoons water
1 teaspoon vanilla
1/2 cup barley flour
3 tablespoons carob powder
1 tablespoon instant coffee crystals
2 teaspoons cereal-free baking powder
1/4 teaspoon salt

Coffee-flavored bars go fine with morning coffee.

In a saucepan, melt the margarine and remove from the heat. Blend in sugar and then the egg substitute and water, beating well. Stir in vanilla. Stir together the flour, carob powder, coffee crystals, baking powder and salt. Stir the flour mixture into the margarine mixture. Spread the batter in a greased 8x8x2-inch baking pan and bake. Spread the warm bars with Coffee Glaze. Cool and cut into bars.

COFFEE GLAZE: Stir 2 teaspoons instant coffee crystals into 2 teaspoons water until the crystals dissolve. Stir in 3/4 cup sifted confectioner's sugar. Stir in enough water (about 1 teaspoon) until of spreading consistency.

CARDAMOM BARS

24 squares
350° oven
18-20 minutes

2 teaspoons instant coffee crystals
1/2 cup water
1/4 cup milk-free margarine
1 cup sugar
1 teaspoon egg substitute, plus 2 tablespoons water
1 1/2 cups barley flour
3 3/4 teaspoons cereal-free baking powder
1/2 teaspoon ground cardamom
1/4 teaspoon baking soda
1/8 teaspoon salt
  confectioner's sugar

Dissolve coffee crystals in water and set aside. Cream together the margarine and sugar and then beat in the egg substitute and water. Stir together the flour, baking powder, cardamom, soda, and salt. Add the flour mixture alternately with the coffee mixture to the creamed margarine mixture. Spread in a greased 13x9x2-inch baking pan and bake. Sift confectioner's sugar over the baked bars. Cool and then cut.

APPLESAUCE BARS

24 squares
350° oven
23-25 minutes

1/3 cup milk-free margarine
1 cup brown sugar, packed
1/2 cup homemade, unsweetened applesauce
1 teaspoon egg substitute, plus 2 tablespoons water
1 teaspoon vanilla
    dash salt
1 1/4 cups barley flour
3 1/2 teaspoons cereal-free baking powder
1/4 teaspoon baking soda
3/4 teaspoon ground cinnamon
1/4 teaspoon ground nutmeg
1/2 cup raisins

Melt the margarine in a medium saucepan and remove from heat. Stir in sugar, applesauce, egg substitute and water, vanilla, and salt. Blend together well. Add the flour, baking powder, soda, cinnamon and nutmeg, mixing well. Stir in raisins. Spread evenly in a greased 13x9x2-inch baking pan and bake, testing for doneness with a wooden pick. Cool in the pan. Meanwhile, prepare Orange Glaze. Spread the glaze on while still warm. When the glaze has set, cut into bars.

ORANGE GLAZE: Combine 3/4 cup confectioner's sugar, 1 tablespoon milk-free margarine, and 1/2 tablespoon orange juice. Mix until smooth and spreadable; you may add more orange juice if necessary.

CURRANT BARS

24 squares
350° oven
30 minutes

2 cups barley flour
5 teaspoons cereal-free baking powder
3/4 teaspoon baking soda
1/2 teaspoon salt
1 teaspoon ground cinnamon
1/2 teaspoon powdered cloves
1/4 teaspoon ground nutmeg
1/4 teaspoon mace
1/8 teaspoon allspice
1 cup currants
    boiling water
1 (1/4 lb.) stick milk-free margarine
1/2 cup sugar
2 teaspoons egg substitute, plus 4 tablespoons water
1/2 cup molasses

 Stir together the flour, baking powder, soda, salt, and spices. Place the currants in a small bowl and cover with boiling water. Let stand a few minutes. Drain the currants and dry them on paper toweling. Cream the margarine; add the sugar, beating well. Add 1 teaspoon egg substitute and 2 tablespoons of water and beat. Add the second teaspoon egg substitute and water and beat until smooth. Blend in the molasses. Mix in the flour mixture, beating only until combined. Stir in currants. Spread in greased 13x9x2-inch baking pan. Bake. Remove the pan from the oven and prepare the glaze. Pour the glaze over the hot cake and spread it with a pastry brush to cover. Let the cake stand so the glaze can dry.

CONFECTIONER'S GLAZE: Combine 1 1/2 cups confectioner's sugar, 2 tablespoons melted milk-free margarine, and 1/2 teaspoon vanilla. Beat on low speed while gradually adding 3 tablespoons boiling water. Use only enough water to make the mixture the consistency of a medium-thick cream sauce. You may add up to 1 more tablespoon boiling water.

VARIATION: RAISIN BARS: Use 1 cup of raisins instead of the 1 cup of currants.

FUDGY NON-BROWNIES

16 squares
350° oven
30 minutes

1/2 cup milk-free margarine
6 tablespoons powdered carob, plus 2 tablespoons water
2 teaspoons egg substitute, plus 4 tablespoons water
1 1/4 teaspoons vanilla
3/4 cup barley flour

In a saucepan, melt the margarine; stir in the carob powder and water. Remove from heat and stir in sugar. Blend in 1 teaspoon egg substitute and 2 tablespoons water. Blend in the second teaspoon egg substitute and water. Add the vanilla. Stir in the flour and mix well. Spread in a greased 8x8x2-inch baking pan and bake. Cool in pan and cut into squares.

Rolled Cookies

GINGER SPICE COOKIES

48 4-inch cookies
350° oven
10-12 minutes

1 tablespoon white vinegar
1 cup milk-free margarine
1 cup molasses
1 cup sugar
6 cups barley flour
1 teaspoon ground cinnamon
1 teaspoon ground ginger
1 teaspoon baking soda
7 teaspoons cereal-free baking powder
1/2 teaspoon salt
2 teaspoons egg substitute, plus 4 tablespoons water

The dough for these spicy cookies can be made up to a week ahead of time and stored in the refrigerator.

Combine vinegar, margarine, molasses and sugar in a saucepan over medium heat and bring to a boil, stirring for 2 minutes. Let cool. In a large bowl, stir together the flour, spices, soda, baking powder and salt. Beat the 2 teaspoons of egg substitute and water into the cooled molasses mixture. Blend the molasses mixture into the flour mixture. Wrap and chill until firm, at least 2 hours. With a barley-floured rolling pin on a lightly barley-floured board, roll out a portion of the dough at a time until about 3/4-inch thick. Cut with a barley-floured 4-inch cookie cutter, and place on lightly greased baking sheets. Bake and then cool on racks.

ARROWROOT WAFERS

46 cookies
350° oven
10-15 minutes

1/2 cup arrowroot
1 cup barley flour
1/4 teaspoon salt
2 tablespoons milk-free margarine
1/2 teaspoon vanilla
1/3 cup sugar
2 teaspoons egg substitute, plus 4 tablespoons water

Stir together arrowroot, flour, and salt. Cream together the margarine, vanilla and sugar until smooth. Add 1 teaspoon egg substitute and 2 tablespoons of water and beat. Add the second teaspoon egg substitute and water and beat until well mixed. Gradually, add the flour mixture. Dough will be soft and sticky. Place the dough in a covered, airtight container and freeze for 3 hours—not more. Flour a pastry cloth and a rolling pin with barley flour. Working with half the dough at a time, place it on the floured cloth. Turn it over to flour all sides. Work quickly as the dough becomes sticky as it warms. Roll the dough as thinly as you can and cut with a 2 1/2-inch round cutter. Transfer to foil-covered cookie sheets and bake. Cookies will be pale. Place on racks to cool.

LEMON COOKIES

36 cookies
350° oven
10-12 minutes

1 cup milk-free margarine
2 cups sugar
2 teaspoons egg substitute, plus 4 tablespoons water
2 tablespoons lemon juice
1 tablespoon water
1 teaspoon grated lemon peel
1 teaspoon vanilla
5 cups barley flour
12 1/2 teaspoons cereal-free baking powder
1/2 teaspoon salt

The dough for these fragrant cookies can be stored in the refrigerator for up to a week ahead of time. After baking, they can be frozen.

In a large bowl, beat margarine and sugar together until light and fluffy. Beat in egg substitute and water, lemon juice, water, peel and vanilla. In a second bowl, stir together the remaining ingredients. Add to creamed mixture and mix well to blend. Wrap and chill the dough until firm, at least 2 hours. Flour a rolling pin and board with barley flour and roll out a portion of the dough at a time to about 3/8-inch thick. Cut dough with large, floured cookie cutters—about 4 inches in diameter. Place slightly apart on lightly greased baking sheets. Bake until the edges are golden and cool on racks. Store in airtight containers.

BROWN SUGAR CUT-OUTS

15 to 28 cookies,
350° oven
8-10 minutes

1/2 cup milk-free margarine
1 cup brown sugar, packed
1 teaspoon egg substitute, plus 2 tablespoons water
1 teaspoon vanilla
2 cups barley flour
5 teaspoons cereal-free baking powder
1 tablespoon ground cinnamon

You may make the dough for these cookies ahead of time and store it in the refrigerator over night before baking. These crisp, flat cookies are a northern European favorite.

Beat together the margarine, sugar, egg substitute and water, and vanilla. Add the remaining ingredients, beating until blended. Wrap and refrigerate several hours until firm. Flour the rolling surface with barley flour and roll dough to 1/4 inch thickness; the number of cookies you make will depend upon the thickness of the dough. Flouring your cookie cutters with barley flour, cut out desired shapes. Bake on greased cookie sheets 1/2 inch apart until edges darken slightly. Cool for 2 to 3 minutes on the sheets; remove to racks to cool completely.

ANISE CUT-UPS

36 cookies
350° oven
6-8 minutes

1/2 cup milk-free margarine
3/4 cup sugar
1 teaspoon egg substitute, plus 2 tablespoons water
1/4 cup molasses
2 cups barley flour
2 teaspoons crushed aniseed
1/4 teaspoon baking soda
5 teaspoons cereal-free baking powder
1/8 teaspoon salt

Cream the margarine and sugar until light and fluffy. Blend in the egg substitute and water and the molasses. Stir together the remaining ingredients and blend into the creamed mixture. Cover dough and chill 3 to 4 hours. On a lightly barley-floured surface, roll out the chilled dough, 1/4-inch thickness. Cut into desired shapes. Place on greased cookie sheets and bake. Cool on racks.

CAROB CHIP SURPRISE

18 cookies
425° oven
10 minutes

1 3/4 cups barley flour
1/2 teaspoon salt
1/4 teaspoon baking soda
1 (1/4 lb.) stick milk-free margarine
1/2 teaspoon vanilla
2 tablespoons sugar
1/4 cup dark brown sugar, packed
1 teaspoon egg substitute, plus 1 tablespoon water
1/3 cup carob chips

The surprise is the carob chips hidden between two brown-sugar cookies.

Stir together the flour, salt and soda. Cream the margarine. Add the vanilla and both sugars to the creamed margarine and beat well. Beat in the egg substitute and water; on low speed, gradually add the dry ingredients. Tear off 2 pieces of wax paper, each about 16 to 18 inches long. Place the dough on 1 piece and flatten it slightly. Cover with the other piece. Take a rolling pin and roll over the wax paper until the dough is about 1/8-inch thick (and about 14 inches long). Transfer the dough to the refrigerator or freezer until it is firm enough to cut or handle. This takes only a few moments in the freezer. Pull off the top piece of wax paper, just to loosen, and replace it. Turn the dough over, pull off the second sheet of wax paper and discard. Cut the dough with a round 2-inch cutter and place half the cookies 2 inches apart on ungreased baking sheets. Sprinkle several chips in the center of each cookie on the baking sheets. Take the remaining cookie rounds and place them over the cookies on the sheets. Seal the edges of the sandwiched cookies by pressing them with the back of the tines of a fork. Bake until the cookies are lightly browned. Cool on racks.

CARDAMOM DIAMONDS

84 cookies
350° oven
8-10 minutes

1 cup milk-free margarine
1 cup sugar
2 teaspoons egg substitute, plus 4 tablespoons water
1 tablespoon molasses
2 tablespoons grated orange peel or grated lemon peel
3 cups barley flour
1 teaspoon baking soda
1 teaspoon ground cinnamon
1 teaspoon ground ginger
1 teaspoon ground nutmeg
1/2 teaspoon salt
1/2 teaspoon ground cardamom
1/2 teaspoon ground cloves

Cream margarine with sugar. Add the egg substitute and water, molasses and peel; beat well. Stir flour with remaining ingredients; add to creamed mixture. Mix well. Cover; chill. Divide dough into fourths; working with one fourth at a time, roll it out on a lightly barley-floured board to about 1/8-inch thickness. With a knife, cut dough into diamonds. Place on ungreased cookie sheet; bake until the edges are are lightly browned.

EUROPEAN HONIES

36 cookies
375º oven
5-7 minutes

1/2 cup milk-free margarine
2/3 cup brown sugar, packed
1/3 cup honey
1 teaspoon egg substitute, plus 2 tablespoons water
2 cups barley flour
1 teaspoon ground coriander
1/2 teaspoon baking soda
1/2 teaspoon salt
1/2 teaspoon ground cinnamon

Cream together the margarine, sugar, honey and egg substitute and water. In another bowl, stir together the remaining ingredients. Stir the flour mixture into the creamed mixture; dough will be soft. Divide dough in half; wrap in wax paper and chill. Flour a surface with barley flour and roll each half of the dough to 1/8-inch. Cut with assorted coookie cutter shapes and place on ungreased cookie sheets. Bake and cool on racks.

PILGRIM WAFERS

60 cookies
350° oven
13-18 minutes

4 cups barley flour
2 (1/2 lb.) sticks milk-free margarine
1/2 cup sugar
3 teaspoons egg substitute, plus 6 tablespoons water

This is a simple, solid cookie, good with tea. It can be fancied up by impressing it with designs.

Place the flour in a bowl. Melt the margarine and pour it all at once over the flour. Beat at low speed to mix. Beat in the sugar. Beat in the egg substitute and water 1 teaspoon, 2 tablespoons of water at a time. Turn the dough out onto a large barley-floured board. Knead, briefly, only until smooth. Wrap dough and chill in freezer for only 15 minutes. Work with one quarter of the dough at a time; keep the remainder covered at room temperature. Flour the dough with barley flour and roll it with a barley-floured rolling pin, turning it frequently. Roll dough as thinly as you can. Cut the cookies with a plain, round, 4-inch cookie cutter or cut it into 4-inch squares. Transfer to an ungreased sheet. Cookies will shrink slightly. Bake and then transfer to racks to cool.

VARIATION: CARAWAY WAFERS: Sprinkle caraway seeds over cookies before baking.

STOCKHOLM HONEY COOKIES

32-42 cookies
375° oven
10-12 minutes

2 cups barley flour
1/2 teaspoon baking soda
1/2 teaspoon salt
1/2 teaspoon cinnamon
1 (1/4 lb.) stick milk-free margarine
1 teaspoon ground coriander seeds
2/3 cup brown sugar, packed
1/3 cup honey
1 teaspoon egg substitute, plus 2 tablespoons water

Stir together the flour, soda, salt, and cinnamon. In a separate bowl, cream the margarine; add the coriander; beat well. Gradually add the sugar, honey and egg substitute and water. At low speed, slowly add the barley-cinnamon mixture, beating only until mixed. Chill dough for several hours in the refrigerator or freezer. Flour a pastry cloth and rolling pin with barley flour. Flour the dough with barley flour. Roll out the dough, turning it to keep both sides floured, to 1/8 inch. Cut with 3-inch cookie cutter; if cutter has scalloped edges, the scallops should be wide and deep. Place cookies 1 inch apart on foil-covered sheets and bake. Let stand for 1 minute after baking and then transfer to racks to cool.

SWEDISH YULE COOKIES

variable number
325° oven
15 minutes

2/3 cup dark or light molasses
2/3 cup sugar
1 tablespoon ground ginger
1 tablespoon ground cinnamon
1 stick plus 2 2/3 tablespoons milk-free margarine
3/4 tablespoon baking soda
1 teaspoon egg substitute, plus 2 tablespoons water
5 cups barley flour

If you roll these cookies 1/8 inch thick, they will be very crisp; at 1/4 inch thick, they will be slightly soft; at 3/8 inch thick, they will be soft. Timing will also depend on the diameter of your cookie cutters. Small shapes take less time.

Bring the molasses, sugar, ginger, and cinnamon to a low boil in a saucepan over moderate heat. Stir occasionally. Cut the margarine into pieces and place them in a large mixing bowl. Add baking soda to the molasses mixture after it boils and stir until the mixture foams up. Then pour it over the margarine, stirring to melt the margarine. Beat the egg substitute and water lightly and then stir it into the molasses mixture. Gradually, stir in the flour. Turn the dough out onto a work surface and knead lightly until completely mixed. Place dough on a barley-floured pastry cloth and turn dough to flour all sides. Using a barley-floured rolling pin, roll the dough to the thickness you want. Flour the cookie cutters, if necessary. Place the cookies on foil-covered baking sheets and bake. Cool on racks.

JUMBO SUGAR COOKIES

20 cookies
400° oven
10-12 minutes

3 1/4 cups barley flour
8 teaspoons cereal-free baking powder
1/2 teaspoon salt
1 1/2 (3/8 lb.) sticks milk-free margarine
1 1/2 teaspoons vanilla
1 1/2 cups sugar
2 teaspoons egg substitute, plus 4 tablespoons water
1 teaspoon water
   granulated sugar for topping

      Stir together the flour, baking powder and salt. In another bowl, cream the margarine. Add the vanilla and sugar and beat well. Beat in 1 teaspoon of egg substitute and 2 tablespoons of water; then beat in the second teaspoon of egg substitute and water. Beat in the teaspoon of water. On low speed, add the flour mixture, beating only until mixed. Divide dough in half and chill in the refrigerator 3 hours. Lightly flour a pastry cloth with barley flour. Flour the dough with barley flour and form it into a ball. Roll the dough with a barley-floured rolling pin to 1/4 inch. Using a 4-inch cookie cutter, place cookies on ungreased pans, 2 inches apart. Sprinkle with granulated sugar and bake. Cool on racks.

LACY SPICE COOKIES

26 cookies
350° oven
15 minutes

1 1/2 cups barley flour
1/8 teaspoon salt
1 teaspoon ground ginger
1 teaspoon ground cinnamon
1/4 teaspoon powdered cloves
1/4 teaspoon mustard powder
1 1/2 (3/8 lb.) sticks milk-free margarine
3/4 teaspoon instant coffee, not crystals
1/2 cup dark brown sugar, packed

Delicious flavor and a delicate, lacy texture—these cookies are guaranteed not to last.

Stir together the flour, salt, ginger, cinnamon, cloves, and mustard powder. In a second bowl, cream the margarine with the coffee. Add brown sugar and mix well. Gradually, add the sifted ingredients. Turn the dough out onto a large sheet of wax paper and cover with another sheet. Flatten the dough sightly with your hand. Then, with a rolling pin, roll over the top piece of paper until the dough is 3/8-inch thick, not thinner. Freeze or refrigerate the dough for 5 to 10 minutes until firm. (You should be able to peel away the wax paper cleanly.) Just lift the wax paper and set it down again. Turn the dough over and remove the second piece of wax paper. Cut the cookies with a plain, round cookie cutter 1 3/4 inches in diameter. Place cookies 1 inch apart (not closer; these will spread) on ungreased cookie sheet. (Don't let unbaked cookies stand in a warm kitchen; they will spread unevenly during baking.) Bake; watch these carefully and do not over-bake. Cool on racks.

GINGER COOKIES

24 cookies
350° oven
12 minutes

2 1/2 cups barley flour
1 1/2 teaspoons baking soda
1/4 teaspoon salt
1 tablespoon ground ginger
2 (1/2 lb.) sticks milk-free margarine
1 cup honey
  safflower oil

You can refrigerate this dough for 5 hours or as long as overnight before using.

Stir together the flour, soda, salt, and ginger. Place margarine and honey in a saucepan and melt over moderate heat. Let the mixture come to a low boil, then pour all at once over the dry ingredients. Beat at low speed to mix and then at high speed for about 1 minute until the dough stiffens slightly. Before wrapping the dough in aluminum foil, pour a little safflower oil over the foil. Refrigerate the dough for 5 hours or overnight. Lightly flour a pastry cloth and a rolling pin with barley flour. Place one half the dough on the pastry cloth and flour both sides with barley flour. The dough will be stiff. Pound it with the rolling pin to soften. Roll out the dough, turning it to keep both sides floured. Roll to 1/4 inch thickness. Use a 3-inch round cookie cutter to cut the cookies and then place them, 2 inches apart, on a foil lined baking sheet. Bake cookies and cool them on a rack. Store in an airtight container.

Children's Hour

MOLASSES BARS

24 squares
350° oven
30-35 minutes

1 (1/4 lb.) stick milk-free margarine
1 teaspoon vanilla extract
1 tablespoon light molasses
1 1/4 cups dark brown sugar, packed
2 teaspoons egg substitute, plus 4 tablespoons water
1 cup barley flour

These are particularly moist and chewy; you'll love 'em.

Turn on the oven to 350°. Take a large bowl. Put the margarine in and beat it. Then put in the vanilla and molasses and beat the mixture again. Add the dark brown sugar and beat again. Add 1 teaspoon egg substitute and 2 tablespoons water and beat. Now add the second teaspoon egg substitute and 2 tablespoons of water and beat again. Beat for 2 minutes. The mixture will be smooth and light in color. Mix in the flour. Grease a 9x9x2-inch square pan. Pour the batter into it and bake in the oven. You can test the bars to see if they are ready to be taken out of the oven. Take a toothpick and push it into the center of the pan. If the toothpick comes out clean, the bars are ready. If the toothpick has batter on it, let the bars bake a little longer. Use a mitt to take the pan out of the oven. Let the bars cool completely in the pan.

HOLIDAY BARS

24 squares
350° oven
20-25 minutes

2 tablespoons milk-free margarine
1 cup brown sugar, packed
1 cup chopped nuts, if allowed or
   1 cup crunchy rice cereal
1/3 cup barley flour
1/8 teaspoon baking soda
   dash salt
2 teaspoons egg substitute, plus 4 tablespoons water, beaten
1 teaspoon vanilla
   confectioner's sugar

Turn on the oven to 350°. Melt the margarine in a 9x9x2-inch baking pan and take the pan away from the heat. In another bowl, stir together the brown sugar, the nuts (or cereal), the flour, baking soda and salt. Now stir the egg substitute and water and vanilla into the bowl also. Pour the flour mixture that is in the bowl over the melted margarine in the pan. Do not stir. It's tempting, but don't. Bake in the oven. Use a mitt to take the pan out of the oven. Sift a little confectioner's sugar over the top. Put a rack over the top of the pan and turn both the pan and the rack upside down. Set it carefully down on the counter to cool. Take the pan away and sift a little confectioner's sugar over the new top. Cut into bars.

SHORTBREAD

10 wedges
300° oven
45-50 minutes

1 cup milk-free margarine
1/4 cup brown sugar, packed
1/2 teaspoon vanilla
1 cup barley flour

      Turn on the oven to 300°. Take a large bowl. Put in everything except the barley flour and beat until the mixture is fluffy. Now you can add the barley flour and blend it in. Take an 8- or 9-inch springform pan. (It's the kind that you can take the sides off when the baking is done.) You don't have to grease the pan. Press the dough evenly around the pan. Take a fork and press the bottom of the tines around the edges of the dough. Now turn the fork over and prick the surface of the dough evenly all over. Bake in the oven. When the shortbread is done, it will be almost firm to your touch and a light gold color. You can cut it into wedges while it is still warm and then let it cool in the pan.

RAISIN DROPS

36 cookies
400° oven
12-15 minutes

1 3/4 cups barley flour
1/2 teaspoon salt
1/2 teaspoon baking soda
4 1/2 teaspoons cereal-free baking powder
1 teaspoon ground cinnamon
1 teaspoon ground nutmeg
1/4 teaspoon powdered cloves
1 (1/4 lb.) stick milk-free margarine
1 teaspoon vanilla
1 cup sugar
2 teaspoons egg substitute, plus 4 tablespoons water
1 cup raisins

These are big cookies, so be sure to leave enough space between cookies on the baking sheet.

Turn the oven on to 400°. Take a medium size bowl. Put the barley flour, the salt, the baking soda, and baking powder, the cinnamon, the nutmeg, and the cloves into the bowl and stir everything together. Take a large bowl. Put the margarine in the bowl and beat it until it looks smooth. Add the vanilla and the sugar to the margarine and beat it together. Add 1 teaspoon egg substitute and 2 tablespoons of water to the margarine and beat. Add 1 more teaspoon egg substitute and 2 tablespoons water to the margarine and beat. Take the bowl with the barley flour and pour it into the bowl with the margarine. Mix it all together very well. Stir in the raisins. Put a sheet of foil on a cookie sheet. Scoop up some dough with a teaspoon. Drop the dough on the foil. As you drop the dough on the sheets, keep each mound 2 inches apart from any other mound. Put the sheet in the oven and bake. Use an oven mitt when the cookies are ready to be taken out of the oven. You can put the cookies on racks to cool.

RAISIN N' SPICE

36 cookies
375° oven
12-15 minutes

2 cups barley flour
1/2 teaspoon baking soda
1/4 teaspoon salt
3/4 teaspoon ground nutmeg
1 (1/4 lb.) stick milk-free margarine
1 cup sugar
2 teaspoons egg substitute, plus 4 tablespoons water
2 tablespoons water
1 cup raisins

Turn the oven on to 375°. Take a medium size bowl. Put the barley flour, the baking soda, the salt and the nutmeg into the bowl and stir a few times. Take a large bowl. Put the margarine in this bowl and beat the margarine until it is smooth. Put the sugar in the bowl with the margarine and mix in the sugar. Add 1 teaspoon egg substitute and 2 tablespoons of water to the bowl with the margarine and beat it in. Then add 1 more teaspoon egg substitute and 2 tablespoons water to the bowl with the margarine and beat. Take 1/2 cup of the flour from the medium size bowl and beat it into the bowl with the margarine. Take another 1/2 cup of the flour and beat it into the margarine. Now, pour the rest of the flour into the margarine and beat until dough looks smooth. Add the 2 tablespoons of water and the raisins and mix them in. Put a sheet of foil on a cookie sheet. Scoop up some dough with a teaspoon. Drop the dough on the foil. Put the sheet in the oven and bake. Use an oven mitt when the cookies are ready to be taken out of the oven. You can put them on racks to cool with a wide spatula.

CLIPPER COOKIES

48 cookies
375° oven
8-10 minutes

1/2 cup milk-free margarine
3/4 cup brown sugar, packed
1 teaspoon egg substitute, plus 2 tablespoons water
2 teaspoons powdered, caffeine-free coffee
1 1/2 cups barley flour
1/2 teaspoon baking soda
1/8 teaspoon salt
1 teaspoon ground cinnamon
1/4 teaspoon ground nutmeg
1/4 teaspoon powdered cloves
1 cup raisins

Turn the oven on to 375°. Take a large bowl. Put in the margarine, sugar, egg substitute and water, and coffee powder into the bowl. Beat everything until it is fluffy. Put all the other ingredients—except for the raisins—into the bowl and beat everything together. Now you can carefully stir in the raisins. Take a cookie sheet. Scoop up some dough with a teaspoon. Drop the dough on the sheet. As you drop the dough on the cookie sheet, keep each mound 2 inches apart from any other mound. Put the sheet in the oven and bake. Use an oven mitt when the cookies are ready to be taken out of the oven. (The bottoms of the cookies will be lightly browned.) You can put the cookies on racks to cool with a wide spatula.

SPICY SLICES

50 cookies
375° oven
10-12 minutes

1 cup milk-free margarine
1 cup sugar
2 teaspoons egg substitute, plus 4 tablespoons water
1 teaspoon vanilla
3 1/2 cups barley flour
1 1/2 teaspoons baking soda
1 1/2 teaspoons ground cinnamon
1/2 teaspoon ground nutmeg
1/4 teaspoon powdered cloves
1 cup currants
   granulated sugar

Turn on the oven to 375°. Take a large bowl. Put in the margarine, sugar, egg substitute and water, and the vanilla. Beat until fluffy. Put all the other ingredients—except for the currants—into the bowl. Beat everything together. Now you can stir in the currants. You might want some help for this next step, but give it a try first; you can always get help later. Divide the dough into 2 equal pieces. Shape each piece of dough into a rectangle about 9 inches long and 2 inches wide. Wrap each piece up in wax paper and put the pieces in the freezer for at least 1 hour. When you are ready to continue baking, ask your mother whether or not you should slice the dough. The dough needs to be sliced in 1/4-inch slices and placed 1 inch apart on ungreased baking sheets. Sprinkle the slices with a little granulated sugar and bake them. Use an oven mitt when the cookies are ready to be taken out of the oven. You can put the cookies on racks with a spatula so they can cool.

VANILLA WAFERETTES

24 cookies
350° oven
12-15 minutes

1 (1/4 lb.) stick milk-free margarine.
1 teaspoon vanilla
1/3 cup sugar
1 teaspoon egg substitute, plus 2 tablespoons water
1/3 cup barley flour

These cookies will be thin, brown and crisp on the edges and light in the middle.

Turn the oven on to 350°. Put the stick of margarine in a small bowl and beat it until it is soft. Add the vanilla and sugar to the margarine. Beat again until everything is blended. Add the egg substitute and water and beat again. Last, add the flour and beat until smooth. Put a sheet of foil on a cookie sheet. Scoop up some dough with a teaspoon. Drop it on the foil. As you drop the dough on the sheet, keep each mound 3 inches away from any other mound. Put the sheet in the oven and bake. Use an oven mitt when the cookies are ready to be taken out of the oven. You can put them carefully on racks to cool with a wide spatula.

CHIPPERS

45 cookies
375° oven
10 minutes

1/3 cup milk-free margarine
1/2 cup brown sugar, packed
1/2 cup sugar
1 teaspoon egg substitute, plus 2 tablespoons water
1/2 teaspoon vanilla
1 cup plus 2 tablespoons barley flour*
1/2 teaspoon salt
1/2 teaspoon baking soda
1/2 cup carob chips

Turn the oven on to 375°. Take a large bowl. Put the margarine in the bowl and beat it until it is smooth. Add the brown sugar and the sugar and beat until smooth. Add the egg substitute and the water and also add the vanilla. Beat the mixture again. Now you can add the flour, salt, and baking soda and beat everything together. Stir in the chips. Grease a cookie sheet very well. Scoop up some dough with a teaspoon. Drop the dough on the sheet. As you drop the dough on the cookie sheet, keep each mound 2 1/2 inches to 3 inches apart from any other mound. Put the sheet in the oven and bake. Use an oven mitt when the cookies are ready to be taken out of the oven. You can put the cookies on racks to cool.

*This recipe works better with barley flour. Rice flour will result in a crispy, crunchy, lacy edge and a soft center; also, the cookies must cool completely on the sheets before removal.

CHIPPERS II

48 cookies
375º oven
10-13 minutes

1 cup brown sugar, packed
1 cup sugar
1 cup milk-free margarine
3 teaspoons egg substitute, plus 6 tablespoons water
3 1/2 cups barley flour
1 teaspoon salt
2 teaspoons baking soda
2 teaspoons cream of tartar
1 teaspoon vanilla
1 1/2 cups carob chips

Turn the oven on to 375º. Take a large bowl. Put the brown sugar and the sugar and margarine into the bowl and beat until smooth. Add the egg substitute and the 6 tablespoons of water to the margarine mixture and beat. Take a medium size bowl. Put the flour, salt, baking soda, and cream of tarter into the bowl and stir everything together. Pour the stirred flour into the large bowl with the margarine and beat until smooth. Add the vanilla and the carob chips and mix everything together. Grease a cookie sheet very well. Scoop up some dough with a teaspoon. Drop the dough on the sheet. Put the sheet in the oven and bake. Use an oven mitt when the cookies are ready to be taken out of the oven. (Secret: take the cookies out just before they look done.) You can put the cookies on racks to cool.

VICTORIAN SUGARS

50 cookies
350° oven
7-9 minutes

1 cup milk-free margarine
1 1/2 cups sugar
1 1/4 teaspoons vanilla
1 teaspoon orange extract
3 teaspoons egg substitute, plus 6 tablespoons water
3 3/4 cups barley flour
   dash salt
9 1/2 teaspoons cereal-free baking powder
3/4 teaspoon baking soda

These are plan-ahead cookies. You can make the dough today and bake the cookies tomorrow.

Turn on the oven to 350°. Take a large bowl. Put in margarine, sugar, vanilla, orange extract, and egg substitute and water. Beat until light and fluffy. Now put in the barley flour, a dash of salt, the baking powder and the baking soda. Beat until everything is well blended. Take about half of the dough, wrap it in wax paper and put it into the refrigerator. Do the same with the rest of the dough. It will take several hours before the dough is firm. You might want to wait until the next day to bake. Sprinkle barley flour on your work area. Take one of the dough packages and unwrap. Place it on the barley flour. With a rolling pin dusted with barley flour, roll the dough until it is about 1/4-inch thick. Pick out your favorite cookie cutter shapes and sprinkle some barley flour on them. Cut out the cookies. Grease a cookie sheet. Put the cookie shapes 1 1/2-inches apart on the cookie sheet. You can scrunch up the dough scraps and roll them out again to make more cookie shapes. You can also use the second packet of dough or save it for another time soon. Bake the cookies. Watch them carefully because the time depends on how thick they are. They will take longer if they are very thick. They will be pale in color when they are done. Use a mitt to take them out of the oven and let them cool on racks.

NO PEANUTS BRITTLE BARS

32 bars
375° oven
20-25 minutes

2 (1/2 lb.) sticks milk-free margarine
1 cup sugar
2 cups barley flour

These bars are hard and crunchy like brittle candy.

Turn the oven on to 375°. Take a large bowl. Put the margarine in and beat it until it is fluffy. Add the sugar and beat that in, too. Now add the flour and mix that in. Put the dough into a 15½x10½x1-inch baking pan. If you dip your fingers into barley flour, you can spread the dough in the pan more easily. Bake in the oven until the color is golden brown. Use a mitt to take the pan out of the oven. Let the pan cool for about 5 minutes and then cut into bars. Put the bars on racks to let them cool completely.

Company Cookies

DOUBLE DAZZLES

48 single cookies or
24 sandwich cookies
350° oven
12-15 minutes

3/4 cup milk-free margarine
1/2 cup sugar
1 teaspoon egg substitute, plus 2 tablespoons water
1 teaspoon vanilla
2 cups barley flour
5 teaspoons cereal-free baking powder
1/2 teaspoon salt
1/2 cup flaked coconut, optional

We need many magnificent adjectives to describe these versatile cookies. They are excellent as plain, single cookies, as sanwiches with a cream-like filling, or even with a jam filling, again as sandwiches.

Combine the margarine, sugar, egg substitute and water and vanilla; beat at high speec until light and fluffy. Stir together the flour, baking powder, and salt. Add the flour mixture and the coconut, if used, to the creamed margarine, blending well. Using a rounded teaspoonful of dough, shape into balls and place each on greased cookie sheets. Flatten the rounds with the bottom of the tines of a floured fork. Bake until golden. Let cool on racks. You may stop here, or make the sandwiches.

CREAM-LIKE FILLING: Beat 1/4 cup milk-free margarine 3/4 cup sifted confectioner's sugar, 2 teaspoons water, and 1/2 teaspoon vanilla together until well blended. Place 1 teaspoon of the filling on the center of the smooth side of half of the cookies. Top with the remaining cookies, rough side outside. Press cookies together lightly.

(continued)

JAM FILLING: Place 1 teaspoon jam on the center of the smooth side of half the cookies and top with the remaining cookies, rough side outside. Press cookies together lightly.

THE DAZZLE: Place 1 teaspoon of the Cream-like Filling onto the centers of the smooth side of half of the cookies. Place 1 teaspoon of jam on the centers of the smooth sides of the other half of the cookies. Press two different cookies together lightly.

COFFEE N' DATE BARS

32 squares
350° oven
35 minutes

1 1/4 cups barley flour
2 tablespoons coffee powder
3 1/2 teaspoons cereal-free baking powder
1/4 teaspoon salt
3 teaspoons egg substitute, plus 6 tablespoons water
1 cup sugar
1/2 cup pitted dates, finely chopped

Stir together the flour, coffee, baking powder and salt. Beat the egg substitute and water. Add the sugar slowly, beating at high speed until thick. Stir in the dates. Sprinkle flour mixture over and fold in. Spread in a 13x9x2-inch baking pan and bake. Test for doneness with a wooden pick. Cool in pan on a wire rack.

CAROB PUFFS

18 cookies
375° oven
12-15 minutes

2 cups barley flour, stirred
1/2 teaspoon baking soda
   pinch of salt
1 (1/4 lb.) stick milk-free margarine
6 tablespoons powdered carob, plus 2 tablespoons water
1 cup brown sugar, packed
1 teaspoon egg substitute, plus 2 tablespoons water
1 teaspoon vanilla extract
1/2 cup water

These big powder puff cookies have an excellent flavor. No time for glazing? Dust with confectioner's sugar.

Stir together the flour, baking soda and salt and set aside. Place the margarine in a heavy saucepan with the powdered carob and water and cook over low heat until the margarine is melted. Remove from the heat. Stir in sugar and then the egg substitute with water and the vanilla. Keep stirring until the mixture is smooth. Stir in half of the flour mixture. A few drops at a time, very gradually stir in the 1/2 cup of water and then add the remaining flour mixture, stirring until completely smooth. Drop by the heaping tablespoonful, three inches apart, on an aluminum foil-covered cookie sheet and bake. Let stand 1 minute before cooling completely on a rack.

CAROB GLAZE: Melt 3 tablespoons powdered carob, 1 tablespoon water, and 1 tablespoon milk-free margarine over hot water in a double boiler. Stir in 3 1/2 tablespoons water. Add 1 cup sifted confectioner's sugar and stir until smooth. Adjust consistency with water or sugar. You are aiming towards a heavy, cream-like consistency. Spread the glaze over the tops of the cooled cookies with a metal spatula. Let the glaze dry, about 1 hour.

CARRES A L'ORANGE

32 squares
350° oven
20-25 minutes

1/2 cup milk-free margarine
2 cups dark brown sugar, packed
3 teaspoons egg substitute, plus 6 tablespoons water
1 teaspoon vanilla
2 tablespoons grated orange peel
1/4 teaspoon salt
2 1/2 cups barley flour
6 1/4 teaspoons cereal-free baking powder
2 cups carob chips

The fragrance and the combination of carob and orange are delightful.

Beat together the margarine, sugar, egg substitute and water, vanilla, peel, and salt until light and fluffy. Add flour and baking powder, beating until blended. Stir in carob pieces. Spread batter evenly in foil-lined 15½x10½x2-inch pan. Bake until golden brown. Let cool in pan.

HOLIDAY LOGS

36 cookies
325° oven
15-20 minutes

1 cup milk-free margarine
1/3 cup sugar
2 teaspoons brandy, optional
   or brandy extract, optional
2 teaspoons vanilla
1/4 teaspoon salt
2 cups barley flour
   sifted confectioner's sugar

Beat together the margarine and sugar until light and fluffy. Beat in brandy, if using, vanilla, and salt. Add flour and beat to blend. Shape dough into small logs, each about 2 1/2 inches long and 1/2 inch in diameter. Place 2 inches apart on ungreased baking sheets. Bake and cool on racks. While still slightly warm, roll in confectioner's sugar. Continue cooling. Frost one end of cooled cookie with Carob Icing.

CAROB ICING: Place 1 1/2 cups sifted confectioner's sugar, 1/2 cup powdered carob, and a pinch of salt into a mixing bowl. Melt 5 1/3 tablespoons milk-free margarine and pour it, along with 3 tablespoons boiling water, into the mixing bowl. Beat until smooth. The icing should be thick enough not to run. Adjust the consistency with water or sugar. Spoon the icing onto 1 end of the cooled cookie (or all of the cookie, if you wish) and let set for a few hours.

SPICED TEA CAKES

30 cookies
350° oven
15-17 minutes

1/4 cup safflower oil
1 teaspoon egg substitute, plus 2 tablespoons water
3/4 cup sugar
1/2 cup cooked, fresh pumpkin
  or canned pumpkin
1/4 cup water
3/4 cup barley flour
1/2 teaspoon baking soda
2 teaspoons cereal-free baking powder
  dash salt
1/4 teaspoon ground cinnamon
1/4 teaspoon powdered cloves
1/4 teaspoon ground nutmeg
1/2 cup pitted dates, chopped

Moist and delicious, these little "bonbons" are hard to pass by.

Line 30 miniature muffin cups with 1 1/2-inch bonbon papers. Combine the oil, the egg substitute and water, the sugar, the pumpkin, and the 1/4 cup water. Add the flour, soda, baking powder and spices, and blend together well. Stir in the dates. Spoon into the paper baking cups, filling about 2/3 full. Bake until an inserted toothpick comes out clean. Remove the cakes from the muffin cups and cool on racks.

SILHOUETTES

70 cookies
400° oven
10-12 minutes

1/2 cup milk-free margarine
1 cup sugar
1 teaspoon egg substitute, plus 2 tablespoons water
1/4 cup water
1/2 teaspoon vanilla
1/4 teaspoon lemon extract
2 1/4 cups barley flour
5 3/4 teaspoons cereal-free baking powder
1/2 teaspoon salt
  Carob Rounds

Cream together the margarine and the sugar and then blend in the egg substitute and water, the 1/4 cup water, the vanilla and the lemon extract. Stir the flour together with the baking powder and salt. Stir flour mixture into creamed mixture, blending well. Chill in the refrigerator for 1 hour. Prepare the Carob Rounds, but don't bake them. On a barley-floured surface, roll the chilled dough to 1/4-inch thickness. Using a 2-inch cookie cutter, cut the dough. Place the rounds on an ungreased cookie sheet. Carefully place the chilled Carob Rounds on top of each 2-inch cookie round and bake. Cool on racks.

CAROB ROUNDS: Cream together 1 cup milk-free margarine and 1 cup of sugar until light and fluffy. Beat in 1 teaspoon egg substitute plus 2 tablespoons water. Blend in 6 tablespoons carob powder, 2 tablespoons water, and 1 teaspoon vanilla. Stir together 2 cups of barley flour and 1/2 teaspoon salt and add this flour mixture to the creamed mixture, blending well. Pack half the dough at a time in a cookie press. Press out, using desired shapes, onto an ungreased cookie sheet. Chill the unbaked cookies until firm, about 15 minutes.

CROSTOLI

24-36 cookies

1 1/2 cups barley flour
3 3/4 teaspoons cereal-free baking powder
1/4 teaspoon salt
1/3 cup water
1 1/4 tablespoons brandy, optional
   or brandy flavoring
1 tablespoon sugar
1 tablespoon milk-free margarine, melted and cooled
1 teaspoon grated lemon rind
1 teaspoon egg substitute, plus 1 tablespoon water
   safflower oil
   confectioner's sugar

The number of cookies depends on how thinly you roll the dough.

Stir together the flour, baking powder, and salt. In a small bowl, beat together with a fork the water, brandy, sugar, margarine, lemon rind, and egg substitute and water. Add this margarine mixture to flour mixture and beat thoroughly. Shape the dough into a ball and turn out on a lightly barley-floured surface. Knead the dough gently until smooth, about 20 minutes. Roll the dough into a rectangle, as thinly as workable, and cut it into 1x2-inch strips with either a pastry wheel or a knife. Cut a 1/2-inch slit lengthwise in the center of each strip of dough. Pour 2 inches of oil into a large saucepan and heat to 375°. Fry Crostoli until golden, about 2 minutes, and drain on paper toweling. Dust with confectioner's sugar.

FRENCH FANS

32 cookies
375° oven
7-10 minutes

2 cups barley flour
5 teaspoons cereal-free baking powder
1/4 teaspoon salt
1 (1/4 lb.) stick plus 2 2/3 tablespoons milk-free margarine
1/2 teaspoon vanilla
3/4 cup sugar
1 teaspoon egg substitute, plus 2 tablespoons water
4 teaspoons water
  grated rind of 1 lemon
  granulated sugar

These are the graceful cookies you see pressed into scoops of ice-cream.

Stir together the flour, baking powder and salt. Cream the margarine and then beat in the vanilla and sugar. Add the egg substitute and water, the 4 teaspoons of water, and the lemon rind, beating well. Slowly add the flour mixture. Divide the dough into fourths, wrapping each piece in wax paper. Refrigerate for 1 hour. Flour a pastry cloth and rolling pin with barley flour. Use 1 packet of dough at a time, leaving the others in the refrigerator. Flour both sides of the dough and roll into a circle about 1/8-inch thick and as large as you can. Use a fluted pastry wheel or a knife and cut as large a circle as possible. With a knife, cut the circle into 8 pie-shaped wedges. With the dull side of the knife, mark each cookie with 5 or 6 lines that radiate from the center to the outside edge. Transfer the fans to cookie sheets covered with foil. Keep fans 1 inch apart. Sprinkle with granulated sugar. Bake according to the thickness of the dough. Fans will be slightly colored, not brown. Let cool on racks.

CANDY CANES

30 cookies
375° oven
10 minutes

3/4 cup milk-free margarine
3/4 cup sugar
1 teaspoon egg substitute, plus 2 tablespoons water
1/2 teaspoon vanilla
1/2 teaspoon peppermint extract, optional
2 cups barley flour
1/2 teaspoon salt
5 teaspoons cereal-free baking powder
1/3 cup flaked coconut, optional
1 teaspoon red food coloring, optional

If you can tint one-half of the dough red, you can have a festive, decorative, holiday cookie.

Cream together the margarine and sugar. Beat in the egg substitute and water, the vanilla, and peppermint extract, if using. Stir together the flour, salt and baking powder. Beat the flour mixture into the creamed mixture. Divide the dough in half. Stir the coconut into one half and tint the other half with red food coloring, if using. Cover the dough and chill it for 30 minutes. Divide each portion of dough into 30 balls, keeping the unsed portions chilled. Roll each ball into a 5-inch log. For each cane, pinch together one end of a red log and one end of a white log. Twist the logs together like ropes. Pinch the bottom ends together. Place on ungreased cookie sheet and curve to form a cane. Bake.

DATE SLICES

44 slices
350° oven
25-30 minutes

1 tablespoon powdered coffee, not crystals
1/2 cup boiling water
3 cups barley flour
1 teaspoon baking soda
1/2 teaspoon salt
1 teaspoon powdered cloves
1 teaspoon ground cinnamon
1 (1/4 lb.) stick milk-free margarine
1 cup sugar
1/2 cup molasses
1 teaspoon egg substitute, plus 2 tablespoons water
1 cup pitted dates, coarsely cut
2/3 cup raisins

Moist and fruit filled, these slices are special.

Dissolve the instant coffee in the boiling water and set aside. Stir together the flour, soda, salt, cloves, and cinnamon. Cream the margarine; add sugar, mixing well. Beat in molasses and then beat in the egg substitute and water until smooth. Stir in the dates and raisins. On low speed, add one-third of the flour mixture, then one-half of the coffee, the second third of the flour mixture, the rest of the coffee, and then the remaining third of the flour mixture. Beat only until smooth after each addition. Line 2 cookie sheets with foil. Divide the dough into fourths. Form 2 strips of dough, lengthwise, on each cookie sheet by transferring the dough a tablespoon at a time to the sheet. The strip will be about 14 inches long, 2 inches wide, and about 1 inch deep. There should be 3 inches between strips. Smooth the strips. Bake until the tops spring back when lightly pressed. Meanwhile, prepare Sugar Glaze. Take the sheets out of the oven and slide the foil off. Let stand for 1 minute and transfer to racks, using a cookie sheet as a spatula. Be sure the racks are high off the counter. Immediately brush with the glaze. Let cool completely and transfer to a cutting board. Use a sharp, thin, knife and cut the slices at an angle into 1 1/4-inch slices.

SUGAR GLAZE: Mix together 1/2 cup plus 2 tablespoons confectioner's sugar, 2 teaspoons milk-free margarine, 1/4 teaspoon vanilla and 2 tablespoons milk. Mix until smooth. The glaze should be medium-thick. You can adjust it with more water or more sugar. Cover airtight until ready to use.

SPRITZ

60 cookies
400° oven
7-8 minutes

1 cup milk-free margarine
1 cup sugar
1 teaspoon egg substitute, plus 2 tablespoons water
1 1/4 teaspoon vanilla
2 1/3 cups barley flour
6 teaspoons cereal-free baking powder
1/4 teaspoon salt
   colored sugar, optional

   If you can, you might want to tint the dough pastel shades.

   Cream together the margarine and the sugar, blending in the egg substitute and water and vanilla. Combine the flour, baking powder, and salt and beat into creamed mixture. Do not chill. Pack dough into cookie press and press into desired shapes on ungreased cookie sheet. If you wish, sprinkle with colored sugar. Bake and cool on racks.

FOOD GROUPINGS

Arrowroot: arrowroot
Arum: poi, taro
Banana: banana
Buckwheat: buckwheat, rhubarb, garden sorrel
Caper: capers
Carrot or Parsley Family: anise, angelica, caraway seeds, carroots, celery, coriander, cumin, dill, fennel, parsley, parsnips, celeriac, celergy seed, chervil, comine, gum, galbanum, kummel, ferula gum
Chicle: chicle gum (chewing gum)
Citrus: citric acid, citron, citrange, grapefruit, kumquat,lemon, lime, orange, tangerine, tangelo
Coca: cocaine
Coffee: coffee, royoc, India mulberry
Cola Nut: cola nut, kutira gum
Composite or Thistle: globe artichoke, burdock, camomile, chicory, dandelion, endive, escarole, head lettuce (iceberg), safflower oil, salsify, tarragon, yarrow, boneset tea, oyster plant, feverfew, wormwort, lavender cotton, Jerusalem artichoke, sunflower seed, sunflower oil
Crustacean: crab, crayfish, lobster, shrimp
Ebony: date plum, persimmon
Fungi: moldy cheeses, mushroom, yeast
Ginger: ginger, tumeric, cardomom, arrowroot
Gooseberry: beets, beet sugar, spinach, Swiss chard
Gourd: pumpkin, squash, cucumber, cantaloupe, muskmelon, honey dew, Persian melon, casaba, watermelon, curuba, cristman melon, cassabanana, Spanish melon, zucchini
GRAINS
Barley: malt, whiskey, ale, lager, some liqueurs
Corn: hominy, corn oil, corn starch, corn syrup, dextrose, glucose, bourbon
Oat: oat flour, oatmeal
Rice: rice, wild rice
Rye: rye
Wheat: bran, gluten flours, graham flour, wheat germ, cake flour, all purpose flour, bamboo shoots, pumpernickel

Grape: cream of tartar, grape, raisin, brandy, port, sherry, wine, champagne, wine vinegar

Heath: cranberry, blueberry, huckleberry, wintergreen, bearberry

Honey: honey, bee nectar, beeswax

Honeysuckle: elderberry

Iris: saffron

Laurel: avocado, cinnamon, cassia, bay leaves, camphor, sassafras, laurel

Legume: gum arabic, kidney bean, lima bean, navy bean, soy bean (soy flour and soy oil), wax bean, locust bean gum, carob, cassia, licorice, black-eyed peas, chick peas, green peas, split peas, peanut oil, peanuts, karaya, tamarind, alfalfa, tragacanth gum

Lily: aloe, asparagus, chives, garlic, leeks, onions, sarsparilla, shallot

Macadamia Nut: Macadamia nut, Queensland nut

Mallow: okra, althea root tea, cottonseed oil, cottonseed meal, cottonseed flour

MAMMALS AND BIRDS

Cow: beef, veal, cow's milk, butter, cheese, gelatin

Goat: goat's milk, cheese

Pig: ham, pork, bacon

Sheep: mutton, lamb

Bird: chicken and eggs, duck and eggs, goose and eggs, turkey, guinea hen, squab, pheasant, partridge, grouse

Maple: maple syrup, maple sugar

Mint: mint, peppermint, spearmint, thyme, sage, marjoram, savory, pennyroyal tea, chinese artichoke, catnip, menthol, basil, bergamot, rosemary, horehound, oregano

Morning Glory: sweet potato, yam

Mulberry: breadfruit, fig, mulberry

Mullosks: abalone, mussel, oyster, scallop, clam, squid

Mustard: mustard, cabbage, cauliflower, broccoli, Brussels sprouts, turnip, rutabaga, kale, collard, celery cabbage, kohlrabi, radish, horseradish, watercress, celery cabbage, chinese cabbage, collards, sea kale, pepper grass, pepper cress, mustard green

Myrtle: allspice, cloves, pimento, paprika, guava, bayberry

Nightshade: cayenne pepper, green peppers, red peppers, eggplant, tomato, potato, tobacco, chili pepper, banana pepper, bell pepper, paprika, pimento, tabasco
Nutmeg: nutmeg, mace
NUTS
Beech: chestnut, beechnut
Birch: filbert, hazelnut, oil of birch, (perfume, winter green)
Brazil Nut: Brazil nut
Cashew: cashew, pistachio, mango
Olive: green olive, black olive, olive oil
Orchid: vanilla
Palm: cocoanut oil, cocoanut, date, sago, palm cabbage
Pedalium: sesame oil
Pepper: black pepper, white pepper, peppercorns
Pineapple: pineapple
Pomegranate: pomegranate
Poppy: poppy seed
Potato: See Nightshade
ROSE
Rose: strawberry
Rose Family Subgroupings
Apple: apple, crabapple
Berry: blackberry, boysenberry, dewberry, loganberry, raspberry, youngberry
Pear: pear
Plum: plum, prune, cherry, peach, apricot, nectarine, almond, sloe berry (sloe gin)
Quince: quince (pectin)
Seaweed: kelp, Irish Moss (laxatives, toothpaste)
Spurge: Jassava meal, tapioca, castor bean
Stercula: chocolate, cocoa, cocoa butter, cola beans
TEAS
Tea: green tea, black tea
Borage: comfrey tea
Buckthorn: buckthorn tea
Elm: slippery elm tea
Gentian: gentian tea
Hypericum: St. John's wort tea
Linden: linden tea

Ruta: rutin tea

Walnut: English walnut, black walnut, hickory nut, peacan, butternut

Water Chestnut: ling nut

(Chinese Water chestnuts: Chinese water chestnuts)

INDEX

REFRIGERATOR COOKIES

Aberdeen Crisps 26
Butterscotch Cookies 30
Cardamom Cookies 34
Lemon-Anise Cookies 25
Lemon Delight 27
Olde-Fashioned Icebox Cookies 31
Pinwheel Cookies 29
Southern Sesame 28
Surprise Pillows 33
Tea Time 32

ROLLED COOKIES

Arrowroot Wafers 70
Anise Cut-Ups 73
Brown Sugar Cut-Outs 72
Cardamom Diamonds 75
Caraway Wafers 77
Carob Chips Surpise 74
European Honies 76
Ginger Cookies 82
Ginger Spice Cookies 69
Jumbo Sugar Cookies 80
Lacy Spice Cookies 81
Lemon Cookies 71
Pilgrim Wafers 77
Stockholm Honey Cookies 78
Swedish Yule Cookies 79

SHAPED COOKIES

Butter Cookies 39
Carob Chippers 49
Cinnamon Favorites 43
Cinnamon- Sugar Cookies 47
Coconut Rice Cookies 38
Crackle Cookies 42
Gingery, Gingery Snappers 46
Gingery Snaps 40
Ginger Softies 45
Jam Logs 44
Mocha Fingers 41

Russian Tea Cakes 48
Snowballs 37
Southern Chews 50

TOPPING

Sugar-Cinnamon Topping 43